MLA GUIDE TO
Digital Literacy

Second Edition

MLA GUIDE TO
Digital Literacy

Second Edition

Ellen C. Carillo

The Modern Language Association of America
New York   2022

© 2022 by The Modern Language Association of America
85 Broad Street, New York, New York 10004
www.mla.org

Second edition. First edition published 2019.

To order MLA publications, visit mla.org/books. For wholesale and
international orders, see mla.org/bookstore-orders.

The MLA office is located on the island known as Mannahatta (Manhattan)
in Lenapehoking, the homeland of the Lenape people. The MLA pays respect
to the original stewards of this land and to the diverse and vibrant Native
communities that continue to thrive in New York City.

MLA Guides series
ISSN 2836-5739 (print)
ISSN 2836-5747 (online)

Library of Congress Cataloging-in-Publication Data

Names: Carillo, Ellen C., author.
Title: MLA Guide to Digital Literacy / Ellen C. Carillo.
Description: Second edition. | New York : The Modern Language Association
    of America, 2022. | Includes bibliographical references and index.
Identifiers: LCCN 2022014790 (print) | LCCN 2022014791 (ebook) |
    ISBN 9781603296052 (paperback) | ISBN 9781603296069 (EPUB)
Classification: LCC ZA4065 .C37 2022 (print) | LCC ZA4065 (ebook) |
    DDC 025.0425—dc23
LC record available at https://lccn.loc.gov/2022014790
LC ebook record available at https://lccn.loc.gov/2022014791

Contents

> ⚙ **TRY IT**   89
> 1. Understand what it means to read laterally.
> 2. Practice reading laterally.
> 3. Practice recognizing your emotional responses to sources.
> 4. Address the implications of psychological phenomena on your research.

> ⚙ **TRY IT**   105
> 1. Practice determining an author's credibility.
> 2. Practice determining sources' biases.
> 3. Pay attention to an author's word choice.
> 4. Notice labeling.
> 5. Explore *Wikipedia*.

☼ TRY IT   143

1. Ponder the value of customizing your online experience.
2. Research social media platforms.
3. Practice adjusting filters.
4. Develop clickbait headlines.
5. Recognize how clickbait works.

Acknowledgments

I am especially grateful to the reviewers of the first edition of this book. Their detailed and thoughtful commentary, as well as their investment in the needs of American students, imbues the pages of this guide. I also appreciate the extensive feedback that the reviewers Marc Marin, Danielle Pieratti, and Stephen Staysniak offered ahead of the second edition. I would like to thank James Hatch and Angela Gibson at the MLA for their leadership as well as Erika Suffern and the rest of the MLA's production team for preparing this book for publication. Finally, I am grateful to Dave for his continued encouragement and support, no matter how many projects I take on. I dedicate this book to Avi and Harris, who never knew and can't imagine a world without *YouTube*.

List of Illustrations

Preface for Instructors

Like us, students are bombarded constantly by information on their phones, tablets, and other electronic devices. Helping them develop strategies for understanding, parsing, and assessing that information—that is, helping them gain digital literacy skills—is crucial. This book is a practical classroom guide for students so that they gain those skills and, even more important, so that they understand why those skills are useful in school and beyond.

Why Digital Literacy?

Digital literacy is a specific form of what was once called *information literacy*. According to the American Library Association's Digital Literacy Task Force, "Digital literacy is the ability to use information and communication technologies to find, evaluate, create, and communicate digital information, an ability that requires both cognitive and technical skills." According to the task force, a digitally literate person

- possesses the variety of skills—technical and cognitive—required to find, understand, evaluate, create, and communicate digital information in a wide variety of formats;
- is able to use diverse technologies appropriately and effectively to search for and retrieve information, interpret search results, and judge the quality of the information retrieved;
- understands the relationships among technology, lifelong learning, personal privacy, and stewardship of information;
- uses these skills and the appropriate technologies to communicate and collaborate with peers, colleagues, family, and on occasion the general public; and

- uses these skills to participate actively in civic society and contribute to a vibrant, informed, and engaged community. (2)

The goal of this guide is to help students develop their abilities to locate, evaluate, and use information effectively so that they become the digitally literate citizens described in the bulleted points above. Teaching students to conduct sound research, assess sources, and recognize bias has been a long-standing priority for many of us. While our commitment to this important work has not changed, the landscape has. Never before have students faced such a variety of source types. For this reason alone, a focus on digital literacy is needed.

Another reason, however, is this: becoming digitally literate has implications that go far beyond school. As the final bullet point in the Digital Literacy Task Force's definition asserts, a digitally literate person should "participate actively in civic society." Thus, as we prepare our students for the next class or the next stage in their academic careers, we are also preparing them to be citizens in a democratic society that depends on their informed and thoughtful participation. To prioritize digital literacy is to prioritize teaching students how to read critically—how to navigate and synthesize information that is dense and prolific, and at times distorted (think *fake news* and *alternative facts*)—so they can participate in democratic society as educated citizens.

This book emerged in response to three contemporary threats to democracy: the influence that emotions and personal beliefs have over objective facts in shaping public opinion, a phenomenon that has led many to argue that we are living in a post-truth culture; the divisiveness in the United States, exacerbated by the digitally enabled echo chambers and filter bubbles through which we receive information; and the increased amount of information available to us, which has made assessing the trustworthiness of information more difficult.

Alongside these threats is the stark reality that students, though active users of digital media, are not always adept at evaluating the credibility of online sources. In their study of 7,804 responses from students in middle school through college in twelve states, the Stanford History Education Group sought to gauge students' capacity for "civic online reasoning." The researchers summarize the goals of the study:

[W]e sought to establish a reasonable bar, a level of performance we hoped was within reach of most middle school, high school, and college students. For example, we would hope that middle school students could distinguish an ad from a news story. By high school, we would hope that students reading about gun laws would notice that a chart came from a gun owners' political action committee. And, in 2016, we would hope college students, who spend hours each day online, would look beyond a .org URL and ask who's behind a site that presents only one side of a contentious issue. (Wineburg et al. 4)

The researchers observe that "[i]n every case and at every level, we were taken aback by students' lack of preparation," concluding that "democracy is threatened by the ease at which disinformation about civic issues is allowed to spread and flourish" (4, 5).

The term *disinformation* is crucial here because it reminds us that access to information is insufficient to sustain a democracy. Citizens in information-rich democracies must be able to understand and assess the information that vies for their attention. They must also be capable of engaging with a range of viewpoints on subjects, including those that are different from their own. The digital landscape, however, now encourages an excessive personalization that creates sealed-off social worlds. This landscape undermines the dialogue on which democracy depends.

A follow-up study also conducted by the Stanford History Education Group yielded similar results. From June 2018 to May 2019, the group administered an assessment to 3,446 students, "a national sample that matches the demographic profile of high school students in the United States" (Breakstone et al. 3). The executive summary explains further: "The six exercises in our assessment gauged students' ability to evaluate digital sources on the open internet" (3). Describing their findings, the researchers explain, "The results—if they can be summarized in a word—are troubling. . . . Nearly all students floundered. Ninety percent received no credit on four of six tasks" (3).

For students to develop competency as researchers in academic settings and as citizens outside those settings, they need more than digital literacy skills: they also need to understand why those skills are important. Whereas other guides and resources focus almost exclusively on strategies for online searches, this guide teaches students why such strategies are necessary, what's at stake if they don't learn about and take seriously the responsibilities of democratic citizenship, and what they can do to empower themselves in online environments.

The challenges of educating students in an information-rich digital culture have spawned a range of strategies, most notably various checklists (e.g., CRAAP, CARS, ACCORD) for determining the credibility of sources. I have encouraged students to use these checklists in my own research-based writing courses. To be frank, the checklists haven't always worked. I have been left to fill in the gaps they create and to teach students why and when to ignore the results of such checklists, which are not consistently accurate in the appraisal of sources. Checklists may seem like an efficient approach to judging the credibility of sources, but they simply cannot manage the complexity of the digital landscape. While no effort to teach human judgment is flawless, this guide offers a more nuanced and comprehensive approach to evaluating digital sources.

Whether we embrace or reject the kinds of checklists mentioned above, the ubiquity of information makes developing techniques to manage information essential. This need has changed both our curricula and our role as instructors. As Richard E. Miller notes, the teacher's role is no longer "to play the part of the master of content; it is to be the master of resourcefulness. . . . [T]he teacher models how to think in the face of an endless torrent of information" (155). This guide will support you as you model for students how to think critically and navigate an information-rich landscape.

Features of This Guide

The *MLA Guide to Digital Literacy* is designed with flexibility in mind. It can be taught from beginning to end, or individual chapters can be selected to meet specific curricular needs. The guide includes the following resources:

> Hands-on, structured activities. These appear at the end of each chapter to test students' comprehension of the material presented, to encourage their response to that material, and to prompt them

to practice the strategies essential to becoming digitally literate. These activities may be completed during class time or as homework.

Readings and associated writing prompts. Located at the end of chapters 2 and 7, these support the specific concepts covered in the chapter and give students an opportunity to explore key ideas that inform this guide.

Four sample lesson plans. These appear in the appendix for instructors. Each lesson plan opens with an informal, reflective writing assignment and includes three activities. These activities can be taught in the sequence presented in the lesson plan or pulled out individually and used as stand-alone prompts.

New to the Second Edition

- Attention to the ethical dimensions of digital technology, including privacy issues and algorithmic bias
- An emphasis on how digital literacy can help stem racism, sexism, ableism, and the perpetuation of harmful stereotypes
- Instruction in inclusive research and citation practices to avoid perpetuating systemic bias in academic and publishing structures (in chapter 4)
- A new chapter, "Composing in Digital Spaces" (chapter 10), that offers instruction in multimodal composition and foregrounds accessibility
- Instruction on reading and analyzing data visualizations in chapter 5
- A new section in chapter 8 on avoiding plagiarism
- A new lesson plan, lesson plan 4, that allows students to explore first-hand how algorithmic bias and personalization work
- A more recent reading selection on fake news—"A Real History of Fake News" by John Maxwell Hamilton and Heidi Tworek—and updated references and examples throughout
- Lists of resources—including digital tools, platforms, and software—that can support the work described in the handbook

The Crucial Role of Librarians

As you use this guide, please keep in mind that your campus or school librarian can be an invaluable source of support for you and your students in their quest to become digitally literate. Librarians have been pioneers in the teaching of information and digital literacy skills to students (and the public) and can point you to further resources to support your endeavor.

1

What Is Digital Literacy?

Digital literacy is partly about knowing how to conduct online searches and get accurate answers to questions. We do this every day. An example: you're streaming a movie with a friend and one of the actors looks familiar, but you can't remember what else you've seen her in. What do you do? You search for the actor's name during the credits, then google it. In a few seconds, you have your answer. Another example: you and friends are sitting around arguing over which soda was invented first—Coca-Cola or Pepsi. After a quick search on *Google*, once again, you have your answer.

But what if you're not asking a question with a clear wrong or right answer? Let's say you google the question, "What are the healthiest foods?" You will find that the results show no cut-and-dried answer. There are many answers, some of which contradict one another. In this case, you are looking for information that has been interpreted, and your job is to evaluate it. So another aspect of digital literacy is knowing how to assess information that has been processed, interpreted, or organized.

Maybe you have some strategies to call on in this situation: you might recall a teacher telling you that .org websites are more trustworthy than .com sites. Maybe you learned how to spot Internet hoaxes or use a checklist to determine a site's credibility—like the test with the nifty acronym CRAAP (see Blakeslee):

Currency (timeliness)
Relevance (importance of the information to your project)
Authority (qualifications of the source)
Accuracy (reliability of the content)
Purpose (reason the information exists)

These tools can help. Unfortunately, they are not enough. If you are going to conduct sound research within your academic courses and have informed interactions beyond the classroom—whether viewing or making online content like videos, tweets, and *Instagram* posts—you need additional tools.

According to the American Library Association's Digital Literacy Task Force, you need to be able to use technology to locate, make judgments about, and produce information, and you need to be able to tell others about the information you find. You also need to know how—and when—to protect your privacy and the privacy of others.

There was a time when experts, editors, and fact-checkers were primarily responsible for assessing the credibility of information. But now that there is so much information online and anyone can publish anything on the web, the responsibility has shifted to everyday citizens to assess information and to develop tools for doing so. As the American Library Association points out, "[t]he uncertain quality and expanding quantity of information pose large challenges for society. The sheer abundance of information will not in itself create a more informed citizenry without a complementary cluster of abilities necessary to use information effectively" ("Information Literacy Competency Standards"). In other words, simply having more information at our fingertips does not mean that we automatically become more informed. We must develop our abilities to use this information. This guide will help you become digitally literate in the ways described by the American Library Association. This guide will not tell you what to think or what to believe, but it will prepare you to take on the added responsibilities associated with living in an information-saturated culture.

Principles That Inform This Guide

The nine principles that inform this guide are designed to orient you to your rights and responsibilities as a consumer of digital information and to help you exercise caution and good judgment as you learn to assess the available web of resources. These principles conceive of digital literacy in a broad sense: while digital literacy is a set of skills that will serve you well as you progress through school, it is also more than that. Democracies depend on citizens to be educated and informed. Being digitally literate in an information-rich culture is part of being educated. These principles, then, should inform not only how you conduct online research for your classes but also how you imagine your role in helping sustain a healthy democracy.

Digital literacy is a human right.

You may not think of literacy as one of your rights as a human being, but the United Nations does. Its UNESCO agency maintains that literacy is a "basic human right" that "empowers people in all walks of life to seek, evaluate, use and create information effectively to achieve their personal, social, occupational and educational goals." UNESCO's website explains further:

> Information literacy enables people to interpret and make informed judgments as users of information sources, as well as to become producers of information in their own right. Information literate people are able to access information about their health, their environment, their education and work, empowering them to make critical decisions about their lives, e.g. in taking more responsibility for their own health and education. ("Information Literacy")

So what does this mean for you? This means that being digitally literate will help you make critical decisions about all aspects of your life, from which sources to include in your research paper to which car insurance plan will work best for you to how much exercise you need to stay healthy.

Being digitally literate is a responsibility.

While you have certain human rights, including the right to literacy as described above, you also have certain responsibilities when you live in a democracy. As Abraham Lincoln so eloquently stated in the Gettysburg Address, democracies are "of the people, by the people, and for the people."

To function, democracies depend on their citizens—to run for political office and to elect fellow citizens to office. Being well-informed, whether as an elected official or a voter, means discerning the difference between information that is credible and information that isn't credible so we can collectively make the best decisions for our democracy. Absent, incomplete, or incorrect information—especially if it is intentionally misleading—threatens that decision-making process and democracy itself. Simply put, information is the lifeblood of democracy. Since one of the primary arenas where we receive and produce information today is the online arena, this guide will help you fulfill your responsibilities as a citizen living in a democratic society.

Neither the media nor social media is the enemy.

It's not difficult to find articles and op-eds (opinion-based writing) that blame digital platforms, including social media sites, for perpetuating the circulation of Internet hoaxes, unverified videos, and fake news or for intentionally posting misleading or factually incorrect information. This is because a debate remains unsettled: Are publishers of digital platforms responsible for vetting and verifying the content they make available— or are they free of such worry, merely providing a space for anyone to make available any legal content? The answer to this question is important. The spread of false information not only has real-life consequences for people (more on this below) but also undercuts legitimate news sources by making people skeptical of everything. For example, a 2020 Gallup poll about Americans' trust in the media found that the percentage of people with no trust at all in the media is at a record high, up five points since 2019 (Brenan). This mistrust is dangerous. When skepticism is taken too far, we lose our drive and ultimately our ability to see the differences between what's credible and what isn't. Why? Because everything we encounter becomes suspicious to us.

Digital platforms play a role in spreading disinformation. But the source of the information and anyone lending it credibility by sharing or reinforcing its message play a role too. Instead of being suspicious of the information we encounter, we should be prepared to assess it. Only then can we make informed decisions about its validity and uses.

The World Wide Web is a web
and is best used as such.

The central chapters in this guide teach you how to navigate and evaluate online sources by reminding you of the original conception behind the Internet as we know it: a web—that is, a network or series of connected elements. In the case of a spider web, these elements are silken thread. In the case of the World Wide Web, these elements are all the pieces of information the platform makes available and visible to you, mainly in the form of websites. This guide will help you become digitally literate by teaching you to read laterally (*across* the web from element to element) rather than vertically (*down* a single source) to determine the credibility of sources quickly and confidently. (This method, developed by the educators Sam Wineburg and Sarah McGrew, is described in chapter 6.)

The World Wide Web presents
a series of ongoing conversations.

Think of the web as a series of interconnected conversations. Describing academic writing, the philosopher Kenneth Burke uses the metaphor of a parlor (or living room) where conversation is taking place. His metaphor describes how this book imagines the web. Burke writes:

> Imagine that you enter a parlor. You come late. When you arrive, others have long preceded you, and they are engaged in a heated discussion, a discussion too heated for them to pause and tell you exactly what it is about. In fact, the discussion had already begun long before any of them got there, so that no one present is qualified to retrace for you all the steps that had gone before. You listen for a while, until you decide that you have caught the tenor of the argument; then you put in your oar. Someone answers; you answer him; another comes to your defense; another aligns himself against you, to either the embarrassment or gratification of your opponent, depending upon the quality of your ally's assistance. However, the discussion is interminable. The hour grows late, you must depart. And you do depart, with the discussion still vigorously in progress. (110–11)

When you are conducting searches and then deciding which sources to use in your projects, thinking about the web as a link to these conversations reminds you to "listen for a while" to what others have said about the subject until you "[catch] the tenor of the argument." Only then should you "put in your oar," or enter the conversation—whether by responding to it directly, explaining it to others, forming an opinion about it, or engaging in some other way.

Unlike people in a live conversation, the websites you encounter may not always directly refer to the other voices in the conversation (although some do, by citing or linking to a source). Still, all the websites contribute in some way to the ongoing conversation about a given subject. For example, a quick *Google* search for the term "health care" yields more than five billion results. Each of those sites, and the web pages that compose them, addresses health care in some way. They are all part of the ongoing conversation about health care. Some sites talk about different health-care plans; others talk about health care in general, both in the United States and internationally; and yet others discuss how individuals can manage their health by changing their lifestyles. The point is that all these sites are contributing to a vast conversation. And it is up to you to make the connections.

If you think about the World Wide Web as containing a series of ongoing conversations in which different perspectives on a subject are linked to one another in a weblike structure, then you will be prepared to take on the work of reading laterally, which will help you assess the credibility of the information and sources you encounter.

Digital literacy is about more than conducting online searches skillfully.

Conducting online searches capably is an important aspect of digital literacy, but being digitally literate involves much more. Digital literacy is about having the tools to

- verify images, websites, and the owners of social media accounts;
- locate defunct websites;
- fact-check websites; and
- use and respond to the information you find online in your own communication and writing.

In other words, digital literacy involves your ability not only to find information but also to read, evaluate, synthesize, understand, respond to, and use that information. Why is this important? As the conclusion of one major research study about students' struggle with information credibility puts it, "democracy is threatened by the ease at which disinformation about civic issues is allowed to spread and flourish" (Wineburg et al. 5).

Digital literacy is essential in and beyond school.

Digital literacy is not something you achieve. It's something that helps you achieve other things, whether you are composing in digital environments or consuming information in them. Being digitally literate allows you to engage in dialogue with other people: writers whose work you are citing in a research paper for class or a boss whom you need to persuade to give you a plum new assignment that will advance your career. One's daily existence relies on digital literacy since so much—including securing insurance, applying for jobs, and even dating—happens online and in a vast global network. If you are able not only to find information but also to think about, assess, and use it effectively, then you are better prepared for success.

Digital literacy can help stem racism, sexism, ableism, and the perpetuation of harmful stereotypes.

Being digitally literate means that you recognize how algorithms used by search engines and websites are biased, as well as how they perpetuate racism, sexism, and ableism and help disseminate harmful stereotypes. While most companies do not reveal their algorithms, understanding as best you can how algorithms applied by search engines and websites collect your personal information and use race, sex, (dis)ability, ethnicity, and other private information is an important step toward digital literacy. It is important, too, to recognize that you can choose to use search engines that don't collect personal information and you can choose to use social media platforms that are transparent about their algorithms. While individuals don't have the power to make these technological systems more equitable, being aware that algorithms are not neutral makes you a more informed user and allows you to take a critical stance toward how and why specific information finds you on your various social media sites and as you conduct web searches.

Digital literacy can stop the circulation of misinformation and disinformation.

The terms *misinformation* and *disinformation* sound as if they might mean the same thing, and their definitions are similar. Both terms describe factually incorrect information. The difference between the two is intent. Disinformation involves maliciously spreading wrong information. Misinformation is incorrect information, but it is not spread with malicious intent. For example, you may have been misinformed about the specials at a restaurant, but it is doubtful that the waiter spread incorrect information on purpose. That waiter was, perhaps, misinformed, and now you are misinformed.

When incorrect information is knowingly and intentionally spread, you are dealing with disinformation. Take, for example, the attack on the United States Capitol on 6 January 2021. Those who showed up at the Capitol were there because they believed that there was an opportunity to overturn the results of the 2020 presidential election. Whether you support what occurred that day is not the issue; rather, the issue is that the people who stormed the Capitol were fed disinformation by then President Donald Trump. There was no legal way in which the election results could be overturned at that point. Moreover, Democrats and Republicans, along with dozens of judges, including judges appointed by Republicans, had agreed that there was no evidence of voter fraud that led to the election results. As such, the claims that there was voter fraud—claims that led to the attack on the Capitol—are also examples of disinformation. In this case, the spread of disinformation resulted in multiple fatalities. If the insurgents had the tools to recognize the disinformation they were being fed, they may not have attacked the Capitol.

How This Guide Is Organized

Each chapter of this guide breaks down key concepts and ends with a set of activities that helps you practice the skills and strategies covered in the chapter. Your instructor may assign these activities as part of your in-class work, or they may be given to you as homework assignments. Readings appear at the end of chapters 2 and 7 to support your understanding of the concepts covered in those chapters. These readings are accompanied by questions so you can delve deeper into different perspectives on the issues surrounding digital literacy.

2

Understanding Filters and Algorithms, Bots, and Visual Manipulation

RELATED APPENDIX ACTIVITIES: 4.1, 4.2, 4.3

This chapter will help you understand how filters and algorithms, bots, and photo- and video-manipulation programs work so that you can be a more informed online user.

Filters and Algorithms

You are probably familiar with the concept of a filter. A filter removes stuff that is unwanted: water filters remove the impurities from our water and coffee filters keep grounds out of our coffee. Similarly, online filters are mechanisms that remove, block, or separate out certain elements. We regularly use filters online. For example, if you are shopping for shoes in a particular color and size, you may set up filters on a website so you can browse only the shoes in that color and size. Filters accomplish this through the algorithms that tell computers what to leave in and what to take out.

An algorithm is a mathematical instruction that tells computers how to perform tasks. Algorithms provide the mechanism by which search engines, social media platforms, and other outlets determine what individual users see online. Although *Google* has never released its patented algorithm, which it constantly updates, we do know that *Google* searches the web for the keywords that individuals enter on its home page and then ranks what it finds, offering users what it deems to be the most relevant sources first. *Google* is undeniably a crucial resource for all kinds of searches because it limits a seemingly limitless amount of information. Although the very existence of search engines like *Google* might suggest that becoming digitally literate is unnecessary since search engines do the work for you, the reality is that search engines—no matter how advanced their algorithms—will never be able to fully replace human judgment.

We do not always know when and how algorithms are applied. Search engines silently apply algorithms to determine which results you get, and individual websites use them to surface news stories, photographs, and information likely to be of interest to you. Social media platforms like *TikTok*, *Twitter*, *Instagram*, and *Snapchat* as well as a range of other sites, including retail websites like *Amazon* and news aggregators like *Reddit*, use filters to keep visitors engaged with their content, including paid advertisements. Filters use your previous engagement with content— what you have read and what you have shared with others—to surface similar information and products. If, for example, you search for your favorite musician, you are likely to be bombarded with advertisements for that musician (like reviews of the musician's latest album or links to buy tickets to the musician's concert). Similarly, if you recently conducted a *Google* search for swimsuits, you may notice a proliferation of swimsuit advertisements on your screen afterward. These examples demonstrate an algorithmic filter at work.

One problem is that the information selected by the algorithm can turn up opinions the user already agrees with. As the researcher and educator Tarleton Gillespie notes, social media platforms "don't just circulate our images and posts, they also algorithmically promote some over others. Platforms pick and choose" (1). So an algorithm might be programmed to select what may be "liked" or shared, since social media platforms depend on posts that are "designed to go viral by use of clickbait titles and hyperbolic claims," explains Jacob W. Craig, an assistant professor of English who studies how writing is affected by technologies. The result is the "prioritization of desirable information over accurate information" (35). In other words, users view only the news stories, images, and videos that the algorithm has determined they want to see, they already agree with, or they will "like" or share based on their previous reactions—even if the information in the posts is not credible. What's more, users are largely unaware of this invisible prioritization carried out by algorithms: a 2013 study found that "less than 25% of regular Facebook users are aware that their feeds are curated or filtered, and even less know how to affect that process" (Hamilton et al. 6). A 2018 study conducted by Pew Research Center found that "notable shares of Facebook users ages 18 and older lack a clear understanding of how the site's news feed operates, feel ordinary users have little control over what appears there, and have not actively tried to influence the content the feed delivers to them." More specifically, "[w]hen asked whether they understand why certain posts but not others are included in their news feed, around half of U.S. adults who use Facebook (53%) say they do not—with 20% saying they do not understand the feed at all well" (Smith).

Sites don't just promote some content over other content; social media platforms have even purposely buried certain news stories. Zeynep Tufekci, an expert on the social influence of technology, analyzed *Facebook*'s News Feed in 2014 and found that

> [the News Feed] algorithm largely buried news of protests over the killing of [eighteen-year-old African American] Michael Brown by a police officer in Ferguson, Mo., probably because the story was certainly not "like"-able and even hard to comment on. Without likes or comments, the algorithm showed Ferguson posts to fewer people, generating even fewer likes in a spiral of algorithmic silence. The story seemed to break through only after many people expressed outrage on the algorithmically unfiltered Twitter platform, finally forcing the news to national prominence.

The algorithm that filtered this news out of *Facebook* users' News Feeds, in other words, was invisible to users.

In 2018, *Facebook* drew attention to its News Feed feature by announcing that it would show "more posts from friends and family and updates that spark conversation" and "show less public content, including videos and other posts from publishers or businesses" (Mosseri). Prioritizing posts from users' friends and family means that advertisements and content from media organizations are filtered out, but it does nothing to allow credible information to be easily discovered.

Filters became an especially hot topic around the 2016 presidential election in the United States because they had the potential to affect how Americans voted. Arvind Raichur, CEO of an Internet marketing company, explains how this filtering worked: "When it came to the 2016 election season, this meant giving consumers mostly content from viewpoints that they agreed with and filtering out opposing or critical content because the algorithm assumed that it wasn't what people wanted to see." He explains further: "Hillary Clinton supporters believed Clinton was winning the election, with no competition, because all the news they saw negated or ignored any valid criticisms. Donald Trump supporters believed their candidate was going to take the presidency because all the news and articles they saw in their feeds told them as such—with no regard for critique or flaws." The problem, of course, is that these filters created a false reality for users.

This false reality has been called a *filter bubble*, a term coined in 2011 to describe how algorithms expose groups of people only to ideas they already agree with and keep them away from ideas they disagree with (Pariser). Filters encourage us to remain isolated from perspectives other than the one presented by the algorithm and limit our ability to make fully informed decisions. By confirming preexisting beliefs, filters foreclose our opportunity to engage and understand others' viewpoints. And because the algorithms instructing filters how to work are both invisible and created by human beings, they also are shaped by bias (Noble).

Algorithmic Bias

Because algorithmic platforms—or sites that depend on algorithms— play such a prominent role in our lives, it's important to understand them, particularly in terms of how they can reflect, reinforce, and perpetuate bias. If you think about it, platforms like *Google, Amazon, Match .com, Indeed, CareerBuilder, TikTok,* and *Instagram* depend on the very notion of bias because these platforms are determining for you what they think is the best or most relevant information or product. For example, *Google* returns what it thinks are the most relevant sources for your research project, *Amazon* tells you which pair of shoes it thinks will be best for you, *Match.com* tells you who you are most compatible with, *Indeed* and *CareerBuilder* tell you which jobs you are best suited for, and *TikTok* and *Instagram* show you content from the accounts of friends and family members you most often interact with.

Researchers that study algorithms have argued that because humans are behind algorithms, "algorithms are opinions embedded in code" (O'Neil) and search engines, such as *Google*, reinforce stereotypes. For example, searches for "Black girls," "Latinas," and "Asian girls" reveal especially disturbing stereotypes (Noble). The bias and stereotypes inherent in algorithms are particularly dangerous because they are invisible, hidden by the seemingly neutral sites and search engines that depend on them. Still, algorithms can have harmful and even deadly consequences. Safiya Umoja Noble, an expert in information studies, compellingly argues in *Algorithms of Oppression* that "marginalized people are exponentially harmed by Google" (28). Noble points out that "while a straight line cannot be drawn between search results and murder," Dylann Roof allegedly reported that his own racist ideas that led him to murder nine African Americans in a church in South Carolina were cultivated by a series of online searches he conducted (117).

You may have already experienced the bias inherent in algorithms if you have completed a profile on a job search website, for example. You are matched with certain jobs depending on your race and ethnicity. Change these aspects of your profile and see how the jobs sent your way change. Your qualifications haven't changed, but the algorithm is coded in such a way that it connects your race and ethnicity to certain jobs. Changing aspects of your profile is one way to reveal—or make visible—the otherwise invisible bias inherent in algorithms.

So what can you do? Remember that algorithms are behind what you see online, and seek to better understand them. Pay attention not just to how you find information but to how and why specific information finds you through social media sites and the searches you conduct. You may also want to consider alternative search engines such as *DuckDuckGo*, which help protect your privacy online by not collecting (and then potentially sharing) personal information with each search. Unlike *Google* and other popular search engines, *DuckDuckGo* and engines like it do not track users, and they return the same search results for each search, for everyone.

Although only time will tell whether the government will regulate the use of algorithms and require disclosure about how they work, some individual companies have come forward to voluntarily explain their algorithms. *Instagram*, for example, recently announced the six key factors that contribute to what each user sees (for more on this, see chapter 10). You can also actively seek out multiple news and information outlets, including those that do not always share your values and views. This will help lessen the effects of bias inherent in your social media feeds and give you a more comprehensive view of the ideas and issues you encounter—empowering you instead of empowering an algorithm.

Bots

According to *Techopedia*, a bot, which is short for *Internet robot*, "is software that performs an automated task over the Internet. More specifically, a bot is an automated application used to perform simple and repetitive tasks that would be time-consuming, mundane or impossible for a human to perform. Bots can be used for productive tasks, but they are also frequently used for malicious purposes" ("Internet Bot"). *Merriam-Webster* also notes that a bot is "a computer program . . . designed to mimic the actions of a person" ("Bot" def. 3).

Bots pose a challenge because they disguise themselves as human beings in the comments section of articles and as account holders on *Twitter* and other social media platforms. They can even spread unverified information.

In fact, Rami Essaid, cofounder and chairman of a bot-detection company, notes that "malicious bots account for nearly 20% of all Internet traffic." He explains that bots have engaged in piracy and spamming, caused websites to go offline, falsified advertising metrics, and even meddled in elections, proving "that the bot epidemic is even more severe than most people realized."

The United States Congress has reprimanded some social media platforms and *Google* for allegedly allowing bots to interfere with their platforms, particularly during the 2016 presidential election, but "social media companies—just like online publishers—have a vested interest in letting bots exist on their platforms because monthly active users are one of their main measurements of success. Accounts, human or not, are accounts" (Essaid). Because social media companies and publishers benefit from bots and because "bot promulgators are anonymous and it's difficult to legislate against those you can't identify" (Essaid), what will happen to bots in the future is anyone's guess.

Because bots depend on invisibility, recognizing them is not easy. Still, paying attention to the activity in an account and the content of that activity can help you determine whether you are dealing with a human or a bot. The number of posts from the account is the clearest indicator of whether you have encountered a bot. More than fifty posts or seventy-two tweets a day is considered suspicious by the Oxford Internet Institute's Computational Propaganda and Digital Forensic Research Lab, which has also determined that more than 144 tweets per day is "highly suspicious" (@DFRlab). Since it is unlikely that a human being would post this frequently, the behavior is suggestive of an automated program. The content of posts is important too. Bots often retweet or quote headlines word for word in their messages and rarely include original content. Looking at a *Twitter* account holder's history of tweets to see if the account consistently retweets and quotes headlines can provide insight into whether the account might belong to a bot.

Visual Manipulation

So far this chapter has focused generally on information and how it can be fabricated, manipulated, automated, and filtered. Visual forms of information, however, such as photographs and videos, pose specific challenges because "we are trained to trust visuals, and so we don't need to use the same brain power, or we don't think we do, to read an image" (Wardle, "Stop"). In other words, we too readily take what we see at face value.

Another challenge is that we rely heavily on visual information. According to the technology-focused journalist Farhad Manjoo, in 2017 *YouTube* reported that people watched a billion hours of content on its service every day. Manjoo notes that young Americans, on average, "spend two hours a day watching video online" and that "more than 800 million people use Instagram, for more than 30 minutes a day on average."

Our extensive experience viewing content online does not, however, necessarily mean that we possess the knowledge to detect visual manipulation. Claire Wardle, the founder of the site *First Draft* and an expert on social media and information verification, notes that visual information like memes "[has] become the most powerful vehicles of disinformation" ("Stop"). While most people are familiar with visual editing programs like *Photoshop*, such programs are becoming more sophisticated, making it difficult for even the savviest of users to detect manipulation. A recent study confirms this: viewers could detect a fake image of a real-world scene only sixty percent of the time, and in only forty-five percent of those instances could those viewers describe precisely what was wrong with the image (Nightingale et al.). As you can imagine, there can be significant consequences if people trust, and rely heavily on, the visual information they see yet don't recognize that the information has been manipulated.

You may think that you are savvier than the participants in the study discussed above, but one study of more than seven thousand responses from middle school, high school, and college students about online information and images indicated that students, too, have trouble determining the credibility of photographs. In the study, high school students were shown a photograph (fig. 2.1) that was captioned as follows: "Fukushima Nuclear Flowers: Not much more to say, this is what happens when flowers get nuclear birth defects." The high school students who participated in the study "were captivated by the photograph" of the misshapen flowers growing near a power plant; the researchers explain that these students "relied on [only the photo] to evaluate the trustworthiness of the post. They ignored key details, such as the source [none was named] of the photo. . . . [N]early 40% of students argued that the post provided strong evidence because it presented pictorial evidence about conditions near the power plant" (Wineburg et al. 17). Researchers were looking for students to challenge the photograph's status as evidence by questioning its missing source or its lack of accompanying information about the person who posted it, such as that person's credentials. Students might have also noted that the post does not offer proof that the photograph was taken near a power plant or that radiation caused the daisies to become deformed (Wineburg et al. 17). The photograph, as you've likely guessed by now, was manipulated, and students as tech-savvy as you did not pose any questions that challenged the credibility of the post.

In addition to manipulating photographs, software that manipulates video footage is becoming more sophisticated and less expensive. Fancy

Fig. 2.1. Manipulated photograph shown to high school students during a study conducted by the Stanford History Education Group

studios and software programs are no longer necessary to make videos, including deepfake videos—or deepfakes, for short. Everyday people in their homes are creating professional-looking videos that sometimes manipulate footage to create products that are altogether new but often misleading. Researchers are also seeing how far they can take video-manipulation software. At Stanford University, for example, researchers have developed *Face2Face*. As the technology reporter Olivia Solon explains, this product can "manipulate video footage of public figures to allow a second person to put words in their mouth—in real time" and combine "voice-morphing technology . . . with face-morphing technology to create convincing fake statements by public figures." Such technology thus has the potential to misrepresent people and their views without their knowledge.

Deepfakes of the celebrity Tom Cruise posted to *TikTok* in March 2021 and viewed by eleven million people (Britton) were especially convincing. The visual effects artist Chris Ume created the series of videos for fun, as well as to bring awareness to this quickly evolving technology (Britton), which, while still in its relative infancy, poses challenges to judging the credibility of visual sources.

Because technology like *Face2Face* is still emerging, it is unclear how you can recognize that someone's voice has been manipulated. Still, comparing what the person is saying to what you have known the person to say elsewhere on reliable sites may help you begin to judge the credibility of the visual before you.

 READ ABOUT IT

In this chapter you read about filters and algorithms. With that section in mind, now read Cass R. Sunstein's "The Polarization of Extremes" and answer the questions following the selection.

Cass R. Sunstein is a legal scholar, law professor, and writer. He has taught at the University of Chicago and Harvard University. He also served as head of the White House's Office of Information and Regulatory Affairs from 2009 to 2012. In this piece, which originally appeared in The Chronicle of Higher Education, *Sunstein considers the consequences of sealed-off social worlds, often called* echo chambers *and* filter bubbles, *that digital culture encourages and perpetuates.*

The Polarization of Extremes
Cass R. Sunstein

In 1995 the technology specialist Nicholas Negroponte predicted the emergence of "the Daily Me"—a newspaper that you design personally, with each component carefully screened and chosen in advance. For many of us, Negroponte's prediction is coming true. As a result of the Internet, personalization is everywhere. If you want to read essays arguing that climate change is a fraud and a hoax, or that the American economy is about to collapse, the technology is available to allow you to do exactly that. If you are bored and upset by the topic of genocide, or by recent events in Iraq or Pakistan, you can avoid those subjects entirely. With just a few clicks, you can find dozens of Web sites that show you are quite right to like what you already like and think what you already think.

Actually you don't even need to create a Daily Me. With the Internet, it is increasingly easy for others to create one for you. If people know a little bit about you, they can discover, and tell you, what "people like you" tend to like—and they can create a Daily Me, just for you, in a matter of seconds. If your reading habits suggest that you believe that climate change is a fraud, the process of "collaborative filtering" can be used to find a lot of other material that you are inclined to like. Every year filtering and niche marketing become more sophisticated and refined. Studies show that on Amazon, many purchasers can be divided into "red-state camps" and "blue-state camps," and those who are in one or another camp receive suitable recommendations, ensuring that people will have plenty of materials that cater to, and support, their predilections.

Of course self-sorting is nothing new. Long before the Internet, newspapers and magazines could often be defined in political terms, and many people would flock to those offering congenial points of view. But there is a big difference between a daily newspaper and a Daily Me, and the difference lies in a dramatic increase in the power to fence in and to fence out. Even if they have some kind of political identification, general-interest newspapers and magazines include materials that would not be included in any particular Daily Me; they expose people to topics and points of view that they do not choose in advance. But as a result of the Internet, we live increasingly in an era of enclaves and niches—much of it voluntary, much of it produced by those who think they know, and often do know, what we're likely to like. This raises some obvious questions. If people are sorted into enclaves and niches, what will happen to their views? What are the eventual effects on democracy?

To answer these questions, let us put the Internet to one side for a moment and explore an experiment conducted in Colorado in 2005, designed to cast light on the consequences of self-sorting. About 60 Americans were brought together and assembled into a number of groups, each consisting of five or six people. Members of each group were asked to deliberate on three of the most controversial issues of the day: Should states allow same-sex couples to enter into civil unions? Should employers engage in affirmative action by giving a preference to members of traditionally disadvantaged groups? Should the United States sign an international treaty to combat global warming?

As the experiment was designed, the groups consisted of "liberal" and "conservative" enclaves—the former from Boulder, the latter from Colorado Springs. It is widely known that Boulder tends to be liberal, and Colorado Springs tends to be conservative. Participants were screened to ensure that they generally conformed to those stereotypes. People were asked to state their opinions anonymously both before and after 15 minutes of group discussion. What was the effect of that discussion?

In almost every case, people held more-extreme positions after they spoke with like-minded others. Discussion made civil unions more popular among liberals and less popular among conservatives. Liberals favored an international treaty to control global warming before discussion; they favored it far more strongly after discussion. Conservatives were neutral on that treaty before discussion, but they strongly opposed it after discussion. Liberals, mildly favorable toward affirmative action before discussion, became strongly favorable toward affirmative action after discussion. Firmly negative about affirmative action before discussion, conservatives became fiercely negative about affirmative action after discussion.

The creation of enclaves of like-minded people had a second effect: It made both liberal groups and conservative groups significantly more homogeneous—and thus squelched diversity. Before people started to talk, many groups displayed a fair amount of internal disagreement on the three issues. The disagreements were greatly reduced as a result of a mere 15-minute discussion. In their anonymous statements, group members showed far more consensus after discussion than before. The discussion greatly widened the rift between liberals and conservatives on all three issues.

The Internet makes it exceedingly easy for people to replicate the Colorado experiment online, whether or not that is what they are trying to do. Those who think that affirmative action is a good idea can, and often do, read reams of material that support their view; they can, and often do, exclude any and all material that argues the other way. Those who dislike carbon taxes can find plenty of arguments to that effect. Many liberals jump from one liberal blog to another, and many conservatives restrict their reading to points of view that they find congenial. In short, those who want to find support for what they already think, and to insulate themselves from disturbing topics and contrary points of view, can do that far more easily than they can if they skim through a decent newspaper or weekly newsmagazine.

A key consequence of this kind of self-sorting is what we might call enclave extremism. When people end up in enclaves of like-minded people, they usually move toward a more extreme point in the direction to which the group's members were originally inclined. Enclave extremism is a special case of the broader phenomenon of group polarization, which extends well beyond politics and occurs as groups adopt a more extreme version of whatever view is antecedently favored by their members.

Why do enclaves, on the Internet and elsewhere, produce political polarization? The first explanation emphasizes the role of information. Suppose that people who tend to oppose nuclear power are exposed to the views of those who agree with them. It stands to reason that such people will find a disproportionately large number of arguments against nuclear power—and a disproportionately small number of arguments in favor of nuclear power. If people are paying attention to one another, the exchange of information should move people further in opposition to nuclear power. This very process was specifically observed in the Colorado experiment, and in our increasingly enclaved world, it is happening every minute of every day.

The second explanation, involving social comparison, begins with the reasonable suggestion that people want to be perceived favorably by other group members. Once they hear what others believe, they often adjust their positions in the direction of the dominant position. Suppose, for example, that people in an Internet discussion group tend to be sharply opposed to the idea of civil unions for same-sex couples, and that they also want to seem to be sharply opposed to such unions. If they are speaking with people who are also sharply opposed to these things, they are likely to shift in the direction of even sharper opposition as a result of learning what others think.

The final explanation is the most subtle, and probably the most important. The starting point here is that on many issues, most of us are really not sure what we think. Our lack of certainty inclines us toward the middle. Outside of enclaves, moderation is the usual path. Now imagine that people find themselves in enclaves in which they exclusively hear from others who think as they do. As a result, their confidence typically grows, and they become more extreme in their beliefs. Corroboration, in short, reduces tentativeness, and an increase in confidence produces extremism. Enclave extremism is particularly likely to occur on the Internet because people can so easily find niches of like-minded types—and discover that their own tentative view is shared by others.

It would be foolish to say, from the mere fact of extreme movements, that people have moved in the wrong direction. After all, the more extreme tendency might be better rather than worse. Increased extremism, fed by discussions among like-minded people, has helped fuel many movements of great value—including, for example, the civil-rights movement, the antislavery movement, the antigenocide movement, the attack on communism in Eastern Europe, and the movement for gender equality. A special advantage of Internet enclaves is that they promote the development of positions that would otherwise be invisible, silenced, or squelched in general debate. Even if enclave extremism is at work—perhaps because enclave extremism is at work—discussions among like-minded people can provide a wide range of social benefits, not least because they greatly enrich the social "argument pool." The Internet can be extremely valuable here.

But there is also a serious danger, which is that people will move to positions that lack merit but are predictable consequences of the particular circumstances of their self-sorting. And it is impossible to say whether those who sort themselves into enclaves of like-minded people will move in a direction that is desirable for society at large, or even for the members of each enclave. It is easy to think of examples to the contrary—the rise of Nazism, terrorism, and cults of various sorts. There is a general risk that those who flock together, on the Internet or elsewhere, will end up both confident and wrong, simply because they have not been sufficiently exposed to counterarguments. They may even think of their fellow citizens as opponents or adversaries in some kind of "war."

The Internet makes it easy for people to create separate communities and niches, and in a free society, much can be said on behalf of both.

They can make life a lot more fun; they can reduce loneliness and spur creativity. They can even promote democratic self-government, because enclaves are indispensable for incubating new ideas and perspectives that can strengthen public debate. But it is important to understand that countless editions of the Daily Me can also produce serious problems of mutual suspicion, unjustified rage, and social fragmentation—and that these problems will result from the reliable logic of social interactions.

"The Polarization of Extremes" Reading Questions

1. What phenomenon is the phrase "polarization of extremes" in the title describing?

2. The chapter you just read teaches you about algorithmic filters and filter bubbles. How does Sunstein's use of terms like "collaborative filtering," "self-sorting," and "niche" relate to these concepts?

3. Sunstein's piece describes an experiment that separated people into liberal and conservative enclaves. One of the results was that these enclaves "squelched diversity." What are the implications or consequences of limiting diversity, and how might algorithmic filters and filter bubbles have the same effect?

Understanding Online Searches

RELATED APPENDIX ACTIVITY: 1.1

This chapter provides you with an overview of the kinds of sources you will find on the web. Understanding the fundamental ideas laid out here will support you as you conduct online research, the subject of chapter 4.

What Is the Difference between the World Wide Web and the Internet?

While the terms *Internet* and the *World Wide Web* are often used interchangeably, they are not the same thing. Believe it or not, the Internet has been around since the late 1960s, while the World Wide Web was only made public in the early 1990s. The difference between the two is that the Internet transfers data and connects computers to computers, allowing us to view pages loaded through browsers on the World Wide Web. The web is simply one of the services that the Internet makes possible. Other types of data, like the music we stream through an app (an app downloaded, of course, from the web), are transferred over the Internet too. Simply put, the Internet is a network of networks, while the web is just one of the systems we use to access the Internet.

Finding information on the web—let alone determining its reliability—can be overwhelming given the sheer range of material available. The chart in figure 3.1 lists some common types of information sources on the web and characterizes their purpose, authorship, intended audience, format, and review process. Keep in mind that the types of sources available online are still changing, as are some of their defining

Fig. 3.1. Common types of information sources on the web

ARCHIVES

Purpose: to make digital versions of physical and audiovisual material available online
Author: anyone
Audience: people interested in the topic
Format: text, videos, photographs, audio
Review Process: often do not go through a vetting process

BLOGS AND SELF-PUBLISHED SITES

Purpose: varies
Author: anyone
Audience: people interested in the topic
Format: text, videos, photographs, audio
Review Process: often do not go through a vetting process

DISCUSSION LISTS

Purpose: to share information on a given topic with a group of interested people
Author: the group members, who are often specialists on the topic
Audience: people interested in a specific topic or who are qualified to address it
Format: e-mail or website discussion area
Review Process: may be moderated, but usually not reviewed or edited

NEWS SOURCES

Purpose: to inform, to provide facts
Author: news organizations, individual journalists or writers
Audience: people who want to be informed
Format: text, videos, photographs, audio
Review Process: updated regularly, fact-checked

REFERENCE WORKS

Purpose: to provide factual information on specific topics
Author: reference publishers or individual specialists
Audience: people seeking information
Format: text (print or digital), audio
Review Process: usually a rigorous editorial review

SCHOLARLY JOURNALS AND BOOKS

Purpose: to present theories and research conducted by experts in a given field
Author: academics, teachers, scholars and other experts, student researchers
Audience: academics, teachers, scholars and other experts, student researchers
Format: primarily text, through subscription databases or online retailers
Review Process: often peer-reviewed[†]

WIKIS

Purpose: to collaboratively create and share content
Author: multiple authors who participate by invitation or through open call; anyone
Audience: people seeking information
Format: databases, encyclopedias, other kinds of collaborative sites
Review Process: because wikis are usually editable by users, their credibility is questionable and not stable

---

[†] A source that is *peer-reviewed* has gone through a vetting process by experts to judge the text's quality and accuracy.

characteristics. For example, when blogs first emerged, they were largely personal in nature and not necessarily vetted by editors or other experts. More recently, though, experts in various fields have taken to blogging, and their blogs can be important information sources; in some cases, blogs have even been reviewed by other experts in the field.

Understanding Domain Names

Simply put, a domain name is the same as a website's address. The domain name for *Google*, for example, is www.google.com. The *www* stands for *World Wide Web*, the middle part (*google*) is the name of the search engine, and the last part, *.com*, stands for *commercial*, which indicates that the domain is owned by a commercial company. While you may be most familiar with .com domain names, there are several others you might encounter, such as the following:

Domain	What It Indicates
.com	for-profit, commercial company
.org	an organization, not necessarily nonprofit
.edu	institution of higher education
.net	organization or company that provides network (Internet) access
.gov	United States government office, department, or agency
.us	United States government office, department, or agency
.ca, .au	country where the site originates (e.g., Canada, Australia)

Noticing a site's domain name is a first step toward understanding and evaluating the information on it. If you want to learn about the courses offered at a nearby university, for example, be sure that you are looking at the .edu web address belonging to that university. Similarly, if you want to learn about the government's guidelines on how to prepare your tax return, you should visit a .gov or .us site rather than a site that is not directly connected to the government.

Finding accurate information by depending on domain names is, unfortunately, not always so cut-and-dried. You should never simply evaluate the credibility of an online source by its domain name. There was a time when students were told to trust what they found on .org sites more than what they found on .com sites because .org sites did not have commercial interests—in other words, their goal was not to make money. While .org sites were initially composed primarily of nonprofit organizations, the designation now includes even monetarily motivated political organizations that hide behind the .org designation as a way to bolster their sense of trustworthiness. So, while paying attention to domain names is helpful, a domain name alone cannot prove the credibility of a source.

Scholarly Peer Review

The traditional form of review for scholarly materials is known as peer review. As figure 3.1 indicates, before publication academic journal articles and books are often vetted by other academics to ensure that they present accurate and credible information, demonstrate original research, use a sound methodology to engage the evidence, and draw sensible conclusions about the evidence they present. For example, an article about Shakespeare submitted for publication in a peer-reviewed academic journal will be sent to Shakespeare experts, typically at least two (if they don't agree, a third review is usually sought). These reviewers write a report to the editor or editorial board of the publication that assesses the merits of the article. The reviewers may recommend that the article be published as is (though this is rare), published only after undergoing revisions suggested in the report, or rejected. When revisions are requested, the author is asked to revise the piece based on the experts' feedback before the article can be submitted for approval by the editor or editorial board. This can be a long process, but it ensures that work that gets published in academic journals and by academic presses is of the highest quality.

To determine if a journal is peer-reviewed, you can filter results in research databases like the *MLA International Bibliography* or look at the journal's website and read about its submission and publication policies. Determining whether books are peer-reviewed is not as straightforward, but presses affiliated with universities, such as Harvard University Press,

University Press of Florida, University of Delaware Press, Oxford University Press, and Cambridge University Press, as well as the publishing arms of scholarly societies such as the MLA or the National Council of Teachers of English (NCTE), are committed to the process of peer review. Occasionally, however, the name of a press will have the word *university* or *college* in it even though it is not affiliated with a university. One way to know whether a press is an academic publisher or university press, rather than a commercial publisher, is to look on the website of the Association of University Presses to see if the press is a member and has therefore met the association's eligibility guidelines.

✿ TRY IT

1. Represent the relation between the Internet and the World Wide Web.

Now that you have read this chapter, describe the relation between the Internet and the World Wide Web. You can put the relation into your own words or develop a representation or illustration. Consider drawing a picture, developing a chart, or coming up with an analogy that helps you explain this relation to someone else. Be creative!

2. Practice keeping track of your daily website visits.

For two to three days, keep a list of all the websites you visit. You could be visiting them for a school project, your own enjoyment, or any other reason. Afterward, review the websites and note next to each one on your list what type of information source it is. You may refer to figure 3.1 above. What have you learned about yourself and your reading habits? What types of information sources did you most often read during that period?

3. Test your knowledge of domain names.

What kind of website is each of the sites below?

www.irs.gov

www.coolsocks.com

www.harvard.edu

www.humane.org

www.news.com.au

4. Ponder the role of domain names in judging credibility.

Is a .org site automatically more credible than a .com site? Explain.

5. Review types of online information sources.

Referring to figure 3.1, which are more commonly peer-reviewed: blogs or articles in academic journals? How would you describe the peer-review process? What purpose does peer review serve?

4

Conducting
Online Research

RELATED APPENDIX ACTIVITIES: 2.3, 3.1, 3.2, 3.3

The previous chapter provides an overview of the different types of information sources online. When you use a search engine like *Google*, its algorithm looks through all these source types to supply you with the information you have requested. As you've probably gathered from your experience with *Google*, it searches the web for the keywords that individuals enter in the search bar and then ranks what it finds, offering users what it deems to be the most relevant sources first. *Google* is certainly useful, but granting it too much power can cause problems, particularly when it comes to finding information relevant to your research topic. This chapter gives you the tools to use *Google* and other search engines so that you can decide which results are most relevant to your project.

Choosing Keywords to "Catch the Tenor" of the Conversation

As chapter 1 notes, one principle informing this guide is that the World Wide Web presents a series of ongoing conversations with which you interact. It's important for you to be aware of how you do so. Once again, here is that excerpt from the philosopher and rhetorician Kenneth Burke:

> Imagine that you enter a parlor. You come late. When you arrive, others have long preceded you, and they are engaged in a heated discussion, a discussion too heated for them to pause and tell you exactly

what it is about. In fact, the discussion had already begun long before any of them got there, so that no one present is qualified to retrace for you all the steps that had gone before. You listen for a while, until you decide that you have caught the tenor of the argument; then you put in your oar. Someone answers; you answer him; another comes to your defense; another aligns himself against you, to either the embarrassment or gratification of your opponent, depending upon the quality of your ally's assistance. However, the discussion is interminable. The hour grows late, you must depart. And you do depart, with the discussion still vigorously in progress. (110–11)

When you conduct searches and then decide which sources to use in your projects, thinking about the web as housing and linking you to conversations reminds you to "listen for a while" to what others have said about the subject until you "[catch] the tenor of the argument." Only then should you enter the conversation, or "put in your oar," to use Burke's words. First, though, you need to figure out which keywords will best suit your needs. Thinking about the web as a weblike structure connecting ongoing conversations will help you identify effective keywords and find relevant search results.

Different keywords will yield different results. Some will yield many results. We will call this a broad search. Other keywords will yield fewer results. We'll call this a narrow search. Both kinds of keyword searches are described below.

Conducting Broad Searches

Say you are writing a paper about the relation between diet and cancer. You might do a search for "food and cancer." Using *Google*, this search yields about 34,600,000 results at the time of this writing, the first page of which appears in figure 4.1. If you review the results, you begin to get a sense of the conversation surrounding this subject. Some sites include information about foods that help prevent cancer. Other sites include information about food that is thought to cause cancer. Yet others outline the foods one should eat after being diagnosed with cancer. With more than thirty-four million results, this search is broad. It can be

Fig. 4.1. Example of a broad search engine search for "food and cancer"

Cancer and diet: What's the connection? - Harvard Health
https://www.health.harvard.edu/cancer/cancer-and-diet-whats-the-connection ▾
Sep 14, 2016 - The link between cancer and diet is just as mysterious as the disease itself. Much
research has pointed toward certain foods and nutrients that ...

Food and Cancer Risk | Cancer.Net
https://www.cancer.net/navigating-cancer-care/prevention-and.../food-and-cancer-risk ▾
Some foods and the vitamins, minerals, and other nutrients found in them may raise or lower cancer
risk.Researchers have studied how certain foods, nutrients, ...

Diet and cancer | Cancer Research UK
https://www.cancerresearchuk.org/about-cancer/causes-of-cancer/diet-and-cancer ▾
Experts think that nearly 1 in 10 UK cancer cases could be prevented through ... Find out the truth
about some common food questions and myths, including ...

AICR's Foods that Fight Cancer™
www.aicr.org/foods-that-fight-cancer/ ▾
No single food or food component can protect you against cancer by itself. But research shows that a
diet filled with a variety of vegetables, fruits, whole grains, ...

Cancer-Fighting Foods in Pictures: Resveratrol, Green Tea, and More
https://www.webmd.com › Cancer › Slideshows ▾
WebMD shows you the foods and eating strategies that may help reduce your risk of developing
cancer.

36 foods that can help lower your cancer risk | MD Anderson Cancer ...
https://www.mdanderson.org/.../36-foods-that-can-help-lower-your-cancer-risk.h12-1... ▾
Looking for a list of cancer fighting foods to add to your grocery list? Our expert says you can reduce −
but not eliminate − your cancer risk by focusing on plants ...

Cancer and Diet 101: How What You Eat Can Influence Cancer
https://www.healthline.com/nutrition/cancer-and-diet ▾
Jump to Cancer Foods - Eating Too Much of Certain Foods May Increase Cancer Risk. It's difficult to
prove that certain foods cause cancer. However ...

Cancer Prevention Diet - HelpGuide.org
https://www.helpguide.org/articles/diets/cancer-prevention-diet.htm/ ▾
Mar 20, 2019 - While there's no magic food or diet guaranteed to cure or prevent cancer, lifestyle
factors—including your diet—can make a big difference in ...

Top 10 Cancer Causing Foods - The Truth About Cancer
https://thetruthaboutcancer.com › Nutrition › Food & Drink ▾
Do you ever eat these top ten cancer causing foods? Learn what they are and four tips for consuming
an anti-cancer diet instead.

overwhelming to see that many results. Broad searches can be useful, though, especially when you are starting a project; they let you see the different ways the subject is approached and the perspectives from which others have considered it. In so doing, broad searches also give you ideas for other search terms, which may be useful as you narrow your search.

Conducting Narrow Searches

You can narrow your topic by reading or scanning sources you found in your broad search and paying close attention to how sources home in on specific elements of your topic. Narrowing your search is a crucial part of the research process. With a subject or question that is too broad, you run the risk of trying to cover too much in a single research project. This often results in a project that lacks depth, which prohibits you from adequately developing your ideas. Because narrower searches often yield more focused writing (and thinking), you will need to create more specific search terms. In our example search for "food and cancer," you can try naming a specific kind of food. For example, a search for "junk food and cancer" yields about five million results, about thirty million fewer results than the original search yielded. The first page of results appears in figure 4.2.

This first page of narrowed search results begins to give you a sense of the more specific conversation surrounding junk food and cancer. The first site on the page discusses a European study that found a link between eating junk food and developing cancer; the study recommends that consumers adopt a color-coded labeling system to make more informed choices about food. The next site lists ten foods that are most strongly associated with cancer. If you jump down to the fifth site, however, you will see that it looks specifically at colorectal cancer (rather than generally at cancer). That's a hint that you can also narrow the second keyword, "cancer," and we'll get to that soon. Let's continue to work with the first keyword we are specifying—"food." We have already narrowed the search from "food" to "junk food." If you would like to narrow the search further, you can do so by considering a specific kind of junk food—say, potato chips. A search for "potato chips and cancer" gets about 385,000

Fig. 4.2. Example of a narrow search engine search for "junk food and cancer"

Eating Junk Food Linked To Cancer Risk - MSN.com
https://www.msn.com/en-ph/health/.../eating-junk-food...to-cancer.../ar-AAAqg5D?li... ▾
Sep 22, 2018 - Junk Junk. New findings from a large, European study revealed a strong association
between **junk food** consumption and the risk of developing ...

Top 10 Cancer Causing Foods - The Truth About Cancer
https://thetruthaboutcancer.com › Nutrition › Food & Drink ▾
Do you ever eat these top ten **cancer** causing **foods**? Learn what they are and four tips for consuming
an anti-**cancer** diet instead.

Junk foods and sugary drinks - Cancer Council Western Australia
https://www.cancerwa.asn.au/prevention/nutrition/junk-foods/ ▾
Jan 29, 2019 - Eating too much **junk food** can lead to overweight and obesity, which is a risk factor for
a number of **cancers**.

Harms Of Eating Junk Food Include Risk Of Cancer - Medical Daily
https://www.medicaldaily.com/harms-eating-junk-food-include-risk-cancer-427567
Sep 19, 2018
New findings from a large, European study revealed a strong association between **junk food**
consumption and ...

Fast Foods, Sweets and Beverage Consumption and Risk of ...
https://www.ncbi.nlm.nih.gov/pmc/articles/PMC5844628/
by RF Tayyem · 2018 · Cited by 3 · Related articles
Jan 3, 2018 - The effects of consuming **fast foods**, sweets and beverages on the development of
colorectal **cancer** (CRC) are unclear. The aim of this ...

Junk food is linked to cancer even if you're not overweight, research ...
https://www.express.co.uk › Life & Style › Health ▾
Aug 17, 2017 - EATING **junk food** such as burgers and pizzas increases your risk of **cancer** even if you
are not overweight, a study has found.

Eating Junk Food Raises Cancer Risk, Even for Slim Women
https://www.theepochtimes.com/eating-junk-food-raises-cancer-risk-even-for-slim-wo... ▾
Oct 3, 2018 - Whether you are slim or obese, one thing is clear: calorie-dense processed **foods** increase
cancer risk, regardless of body weight.

'Junk food' may increase cancer risk in 'healthy weight' women - NHS
https://www.nhs.uk › Behind the Headlines › Cancer ▾
Aug 18, 2017 - "Women who eat **junk food** such as burgers or pizza are increasing their risk of **cancer**
even if they're not overweight, new research has warned ...

How Junk Food Leads to Cancer (& Other Serious Health Issues ...
https://www.youtube.com/watch?v=is2kX4JgHy8

Oct 16, 2018 - Uploaded by The Truth About Cancer
In this video from TTAC LIVE 2017, Liana Werner-Gray opens up about her painful
experience with **eating** the ...

results. Notice how much narrower that search is than the original search that yielded almost one hundred times that amount! The first page of this narrower search appears in figure 4.3. And, if you want to go even further, you can narrow the search to a particular kind of cancer. A search for "potato chips and pancreatic cancer" yields about 362,000 results, as you can see in figure 4.4.

The table below shows how the process of making your search term more specific yields fewer and more focused results.

Keywords / Search terms	Number of results
food and cancer	34,600,000
junk food and cancer	5,000,000
potato chips and cancer	385,000
potato chips and pancreatic cancer	362,000

The scope of your search—how narrow or broad it should be—depends on your project. Usually, though, you begin broadly with general search terms to gain a sense of the conversation surrounding your subject. Then, you narrow the search as you go. In the example above, we began with the broad topic of the relation between food and cancer. But with more than thirty-four million results, such a topic would not allow us to go into much depth in a research project. Instead, the project would likely become a long list of ways that different kinds of food can affect one's chances of developing cancer. The narrower topic of potato chips and pancreatic cancer will allow us to look in more depth at the relation between the two. For example, a project with this topic can explore detailed questions such as, What is in potato chips that may cause this particular kind of cancer? Does the relation between potato chips and pancreatic cancer have to do with how the potato chips are made? Are organic potato chips also linked to pancreatic cancer? As you conduct narrow searches, remember that, as smart as *Google* and other search engines are, they cannot determine the relevance of sources to your specific project or question. You need to take the time to read through the pages of results from the search engine and make decisions about relevance.

Another way to limit the scope of your results is by the kind of website searched. Your instructor may prefer that you use scholarly sites. That's where *Google Scholar* comes in.

Fig. 4.3. Example of search terms narrowed to "potato chips and cancer"

Acrylamide and Cancer Risk - American Cancer Society
https://www.cancer.org/cancer/cancer-causes/acrylamide.html ▾
Feb 11, 2019 - Learn what we know about acrylamide and **cancer** risk here. ... Some foods with higher levels of acrylamide include French fries, **potato chips,** ...

Add French Fries, Potato Chips to the List of Cancer-Causing Foods ...
https://www.mdmag.com/.../add-french-fries-potato-chips-to-the-list-of-cancer-causin... ▾
Mar 14, 2016 - Starchy foods, such as bagels, were recently targeted for being linked to lung **cancer.** Now officials are flagging foods like French **fries** and **potato chips** for containing acrylamide, a dangerous chemical that may cause **cancer.** In 2002, it was found that many heated foods contain the chemical acrylamide.

Acrylamide and Cancer Risk - National Cancer Institute
https://www.cancer.gov/about-cancer/causes-prevention/risk/.../acrylamide-fact-sheet ▾
Dec 5, 2017 - A fact sheet about acrylamide and **cancer** risk.

Settlement will reduce carcinogens in potato chips - ABC News
https://abcnews.go.com/Business/story?id=5503949&page=1
Four food manufacturers agreed to reduce levels of a **cancer**-causing chemical in their **potato chips** and french **fries** under a settlement announced Friday by the state attorney general's office. ... Acrylamide forms naturally when starchy foods are baked or fried.

"Healthy" Potato Chips? - The Truth About Cancer
https://thetruthaboutcancer.com › Cancer Causes ▾
May 5, 2017 - It's very likely that you're already aware of the link between fried potatoes and **cancer** and that **potato chips** are generally considered to be a ...

Possible carcinogen found in French fries, potato chips and other ...
https://www.ctvnews.ca/.../possible-carcinogen-found-in-french-fries-potato-chips-and-o...
Mar 7, 2019 - Foods such as French fries and **potato chips** have been linked to genome mutations that could lead to **cancer,** according to the results of new ...

Do potato chips cause cancer? - Quora
https://www.quora.com/Do-potato-chips-cause-cancer
Jun 12, 2017 - So a once off of 2 bags of **potato chips** would hardly have influenced your intake ... health, even increase your risk of developing **cancer,** thus feel guilty about it.

Are **potato chips** healthy?	Jul 10, 2017
What foods cause **cancer**?	Feb 21, 2017
Does eating **potato chips** cause **cancer**?	Sep 5, 2016
What common food items contain acrylamide - the **cancer** causing ...	May 18, 2011

More results from www.quora.com

Are potatoes now a cancer risk? Here's what you need to know | New ...
https://www.newscientist.com/.../2118565-are-potatoes-now-a-cancer-risk-heres-what-... ▾
Jan 23, 2017 - ... of the **cancer** risk associated with cooking **potatoes** and other starchy ... calorie foods like crisps, **chips** and biscuits, which are major sources ...

It Is Official. Potato Chips are Carcinogenic BUT It Is Not Because of ...
https://althealthworks.com/.../it-is-official-chips-french-fries-and-cooked-potatoes-are-... ▾
Oct 20, 2016 - The National **Cancer** Institute (NCI) has reviewed this chemical and confirmed It is

Fig. 4.4. Example of search terms narrowed further to "potato chips and pancreatic cancer"

Dietary patterns and risk of pancreatic cancer in a large population ...
https://www.ncbi.nlm.nih.gov/pubmed/23368926 ▾
by JM Chan · 2013 · Cited by 38 · Related articles
A Western dietary pattern, characterized by higher intake of red and processed meats, **potato chips**,
sugary beverages, sweets, high fat dairy, eggs, and refined grains, was associated with a 2.4-fold
increased risk of **pancreatic cancer** among men (95% CI = 1.3-4.2, P trend = 0.008) but was not
associated with risk among ...

People also ask

What foods should you avoid if you have pancreatic cancer?	⌄
What are the symptoms of your pancreas not working properly?	⌄
What does the pain of pancreatitis feel like?	⌄
What foods cure pancreatic cancer?	⌄

Feedback

Diet and Surgery for pancreatic cancer · Pancreatic Cancer Action
https://pancreaticcanceraction.org/...pancreatic-cancer/.../diet-surgery-pancreatic-cance... ▾
Add extras to your basic meals such as milk powder to milky drinks and custards, cereals, sauces and
mashed **potato**; add cheese to sauces, soup, vegetables ...

Foods to Avoid With Pancreatic Cancer | Livestrong.com
https://www.livestrong.com › ... › Diet and Nutrition › Special Dietary Considerations ▾
May 23, 2018 - **Pancreatic cancer** occurs when cells grow abnormally. ... such as beef and bacon, and
fatty snacks, like **potato chips** and dips, nachos and fried ...

Ch-ch-chips! - The Pancreatitis Survival Guide
https://thepancreatitissurvivalguide.weebly.com/product-look-out/ch-ch-chips ▾
Nov 15, 2013 · ... in laboratory animals and having pancreatitis comes with an increased risk of
pancreatic cancer. So, don't eat high doses of **potato chips**!

Best and Worst Foods for Pancreatitis Pain – Health Essentials from ...
https://health.clevelandclinic.org/best-and-worst-foods-for-pancreatitis-pain/ ▾
Nov 29, 2017 - Get tips on best and worst foods for a pancreas-friendly diet. ... Red meat; Organ meat;
French fries, **potato chips**; Mayonnaise; Margarine, butter; Full-fat ... meat and red meat increases
pancreatic cancer risk , Dr. Chahal says.

13 Foods You Should Never Eat If You Don't Want Cancer | Reader's ...
https://www.rd.com/health/wellness/foods-never-eat-cancer/ ▾
Close up **potato chips** on wood top view background. ... your risk of developing **pancreatic cancer** by
60 percent, while another found it nearly doubles the risk of ...

Vegetable and Fruit Intake and Pancreatic Cancer in a Population ...
cebp.aacrjournals.org/content/14/9/2093 ▾
by JM Chan · 2005 · Cited by 156 · Related articles
Sep 1, 2005 - **Pancreatic cancer** is one of the most devastating and rapidly fatal cancers, ... potatoes,
baked, boiled and mashed potatoes, and **potato chips**.

Navigating *Google Scholar*

Google Scholar restricts your search results to sources written by scholars—that is, professional researchers. Many of the sources on *Google Scholar* are published by academic organizations and have been vetted or approved by experts in particular fields through a process called *peer review*, as discussed in chapter 3. When using *Google Scholar*, you apply the same strategies for conducting broad and narrow searches described above.

While *Google Scholar*'s search engine limits search results to scholarly materials likely to be more credible than many of those found through *Google*'s standard search engine, do not assume that *Google Scholar* will do all the work for you. You will still have to make decisions about the relevance of the sources it returns. And whether a source is relevant is more important than whether it is scholarly. You'll read more about determining a source's relevance later in this chapter.

Practicing Inclusive Search and Citation Habits

One important bit of work that *Google Scholar* and other search engines cannot do for you is help you cultivate inclusive search and citation habits. Within this context, when you are inclusive, you include—through the sources you choose—voices from different groups of people. Unfortunately, academia, like many other institutions, has for centuries created barriers to publishing for people of color and other marginalized groups. What this means for you is that it will be more difficult to find sources by scholars from traditionally marginalized groups. Still, including sources written by people of color and Indigenous peoples, as well as scholars with disabilities, for example, can help stem the bias in academia toward white scholars.

The sources that researchers, including you, choose to cite can unintentionally perpetuate racism, ableism, and other systemic forms of oppression by continuing to cite only those authors that have always been cited. In doing so, you will likely perpetuate this systemic oppression where the voices of white and able-bodied authors are continually privileged over other voices. Therefore, as you consider which sources to include in your research, remain open to introducing sources that have not been incorporated into discussions about the subject, especially those written by scholars from traditionally marginalized groups.

Committing to practicing inclusive search and citation habits is an important part of ethical research and scholarship. However, because search engines do not reveal biographical information about the authors of each source, you need to undertake some additional work. You can gain access to research and scholarly publications by traditionally marginalized scholars from across the disciplines by following scholarly citation campaigns such as the Cite Black Women movement, the CiteASista movement, and the Citation Practices Challenge. Some fields also publish discipline-specific resources and databases that contain scholarship and research published by traditionally underrepresented groups. For example, the *Twitter* account @EEB_POC retweets papers and research published by scientists of color in the fields of ecology, evolution, and behavior. The field of psychology has a range of resources, including archives such as *BME Psychology* (bmepsychology.com/resources) and *SPARK*, the scholars of color database, both of which provide access to the names of scholars in psychology who are from underrepresented groups.

Locating similar resources in the field in which you are researching will help you enrich the discussion surrounding your subject by giving voice to those whose scholarship has historically remained neglected.

Using a Search Engine's Help Features

While you likely have extensive experience using a search engine like *Google*, you may not know that it offers many tips to help you refine your searches so that you can more efficiently and effectively find what you are looking for. For example, *Google* offers a series of tips to refine your web searches to make them more precise. These tips include instructions on

- how to combine searches
- how to locate a specific domain
- when to include and exclude words from your searches
- how to get information about a specific site

- how to answer specific types of questions (e.g., what the weather is in a certain location, the solution to a mathematical problem)
- how to filter your search results
- how to read the results pages

Google Scholar offers a set of tips on

- how to prioritize the date of a publication when you are searching
- how to search for full-text articles (as opposed to only abstracts)
- how to use the "related articles" link

Take time to review the help features provided by the search engine you use. Doing so will save you time in the long run by producing more relevant search results.

Searching Library Catalogs and Databases

Another digital resource for finding information is your school's library catalog and databases. The library catalog will allow you to search items that you can borrow from your library, including print books, e-books, journals, and magazines. While you may be hesitant to search for entire books, keep in mind that you don't have to read the whole thing. Reading just an introduction or chapter (or two) might be helpful. Plus, books published by university presses and scholarly societies (like the MLA) are usually vetted and approved by experts, so they are likely to be credible. Of course, you'll still need to consider relevance.

Your campus or school library also likely subscribes to several databases. Databases contain information about where to find materials on a particular subject and often provide direct digital access to the materials. There are general databases such as *EBSCOhost* and *Academic Search Premier* that contain material on various subjects, and there are subject-specific databases such as the *MLA International Bibliography* (for literary criticism) and *PsycINFO* (for psychology) that contain materials related only to a specific subject. You can find relevant databases if you search by subject. If you already know the name of the database you need, search for it by name through your library's home page. You can also likely browse your campus's list of databases to get an overall sense of the databases the library subscribes to. Keep in mind that librarians are often happy to help you navigate these databases and can serve as resources throughout your research process.

The library's catalog and databases give you access to sources that are typically more credible than those you will find doing an online search. An online search may yield some credible sources, but it may also find personal websites and similar sources that may not be appropriate for your project. Moreover, if you search through your library's catalog or databases, you will likely have free access to articles and materials that would require a fee if you attempted to access them through a public search engine such as *Google*. For an in-depth look at how to use these resources, including how to conduct specialized searches in databases, please see the *MLA Guide to Undergraduate Research in Literature*.

Reviewing Your Search Results

Whether you are searching the web, using *Google Scholar* to find scholarly materials, or searching your library's catalog or databases, you must consistently review your search results for their relevance to your project. You may not be inclined to do this: studies show that students choose sources not because of relevance but because of ease of use (Purdy). Reviewing for relevance, however, is important. It will be easier in the long run and produce better research results. To assess relevance, review at least a few pages of search results; too often, students stop at the first page of results (Granka et al.; Balatsoukas and Ruthven; Georgas). If you review only the first page, you are relying too heavily on the search engine to determine the relevance of the results for you. Remember that when you're working on a paper or other research project, the algorithm that brought you those results does not know what your assignment is, so only you can really determine which sources will be most useful. Doing research is a process of refining your ideas, so remain flexible and open during the process. And always keep in mind that while a search engine's algorithm will provide you with the results *it* thinks are most relevant to your project, only *you* can make the final determination.

Determining a Source's Relevance

It is up to writers and researchers like you to make connections among sources—that is, to show how those sources are relevant to your project. Let's look at an example. Maybe you are writing about how the media represents the relation between violent video games and acts of violence. First, as we did with the terms "food" and "cancer" earlier in this chapter, you will want to conduct a broad search to get a general sense of what sources say about how media represent the relation between violent video games and acts of violence. An excerpt from the first page of the results of that *Google* search is shown in figure 4.5.

There are some interesting sources in the search results, and they can begin to help you consider a more specific, narrow way into the subject. For example, these sources suggest that one way to narrow your search includes clarifying what you mean by *the media*. Will you be looking at only news sources? If so, what kinds? Will you consider independently published news websites like the site for *The New York Times*? Online news aggregators like *Reddit*? Television networks—national, local, and cable ones? Once you narrow the focus by answering these and other questions, you can begin to locate sources and determine their relevance.

Let's say you limit your search to how a single news network represents the relation between violent video games and acts of violence. In that case, news stories from other networks are not likely relevant to your project. Perhaps you choose Fox News. If you search for "Fox News video games and violence" on *Google*, an excerpt from the first page of results you get is shown in figure 4.6. The relevance of sources depends largely on their content—or what they say. To determine if a source is relevant to your particular project, you need to spend time figuring out what the source is about. The titles and descriptions of the sources that appear on the first page of this *Google* search for "Fox News video games and violence" suggest that these sources are all relevant to the subject, but you would need to read, listen to, or watch them to confirm.

The issue of relevance is a complex one. While you will find some sources that are definitely not relevant and others that definitely are, it's

Fig. 4.5. Example of initial search for the relation between violent video games and acts of violence

Do Violent Video Games Make Kids More Violent? | Psychology Today
https://www.psychologytoday.com/.../do-violent-video-games-make-kids-more-violen... ▼
As **violent video games** continue to grow in popularity, do they lead to real-life **violence**?

The Science Behind Video Games and Violence | NOVA | PBS | NOVA ...
https://www.pbs.org/wgbh/.../what-science-knows-about-video-games-and-violence/ ▼
Feb 28, 2013 - People have turned to science for answers on the question of **violence** and **video games**. For now, though, there are no answers, at least not of ...

Do video games lead to violence? - CNN - CNN.com
https://www.cnn.com/2016/07/25/health/video-games-and-violence/index.html
Feb 22, 2018 - (CNN)President Donald Trump said Thursday during a White House meeting on school safety that the nation needs to address what young people are seeing. "I'm hearing more and more people saying the level of **violence** on **video games** is really shaping young people's thoughts," he said.

Video game controversies - Wikipedia
https://en.wikipedia.org/wiki/Video_game_controversies ▼
Video game controversies are societal scientific arguments about whether the content of **video** .... A common theory is that playing **violent video games** increases aggression in young people. Various studies claim to support this hypothesis.

Children's Violent Video Game Play Associated with Increased ...
https://www.dartmouth.edu/.../childrens-violent-video-games-increased-aggressive-be... ▼
Oct 3, 2018 - Dartmouth Analysis of Multiple Studies Demonstrates How Effect Varies Across Ethnicity. Oct. 1, 2018 – **Violent video game** play by ...

What Research Says About Video Games And Violence In Children ...
https://www.npr.org/.../what-research-says-about-video-games-and-violence-in-children
Mar 8, 2018 - President Trump held a roundtable at the White House Thursday to discuss **violent video games** and how they relate to school shootings.

New Research Finds No Link Between Violent Video Games and ...
https://interestingengineering.com/new-research-finds-no-link-between-violent-video-... ▼
Feb 15, 2019 - Oxford University has found no link between the amount of time playing **violent video games** and real-world aggressive behavior in teens.

It's time to end the debate about video games and violence
theconversation.com/its-time-to-end-the-debate-about-video-games-and-violence-916... ▼
Feb 16, 2018 - For years, there have been questions about research showing connections between playing **violent video games** and aggressive behavior.

Many factors influence video games' link to violent acts, UB researcher ...
www.buffalo.edu/ubnow/stories/2019/03/lamb-video-games-violence.html ▼
Mar 6, 2019 - Exposure to **violent video games** alone does not create aggressive behavior, but these games may trigger **violent** acts in people with a ...

Fig. 4.6. Example of narrowed search for "Fox News video games and violence"

Are video games linked to real world violence? | Fox News Video
https://video.foxnews.com/v/5748074279001/

Mar 8, 2018
08, 2018 - 6:25 - Insight on 'The Ingraham Angle' after President Trump holds a meeting on **violence** and ...

Violent video games increase aggression, desensitize kids? - Fox News
https://video.foxnews.com/v/5748280379001/

Mar 9, 2018
Trump meets **video game** industry leader to discuss the possible correlation. Lt. Col. Dave Grossman ...

Are video games linked to real world violence? - YouTube
https://www.youtube.com/watch?v=29EN9Anic9Q

Mar 8, 2018 - Uploaded by Fox News
FOX News Channel (FNC. ... on 'The Ingraham Angle' after President Trump holds a meeting on **violence** ...

Fox News - What role, if any, do violent video games play... | Facebook
https://www.facebook.com/FoxNews/...violent-video-games...violence...-/101516465... ▾
What role, if any, do **violent video games** play in the **violence** we see in American society?

Donald Trump Vs. Video Games: Are His Game Violence Experts ...
https://www.newsweek.com/donald-trump-vs-video-games-gun-violence-837435 ▾
Mar 8, 2018 - Donald Trump's **video game** meeting, his attempt to address gun **violence** by blaming gaming, brings together a collection of **Fox News** talking ...

Donald Trump Blames Video Games for School Shootings | Time
time.com › Politics › Donald Trump ▾
Mar 8, 2018 - President Donald Trump blamed **violent video games** for school shootings. Here's what the research says about **video games and violence**.

Fox News Demands Ban On Thing That Hurts Children: Video Games ...
https://www.wonkette.com/fox-news-demands-ban-on-things-that-kill-kids-video-games ▾
Aug 28, 2018 - **Fox News** Demands Ban On Thing That Hurts Children: **Video Games**. Guns ... I think that playing those **violent video games** clearly influences ...

Adam Lanza Shooting: Fox News Blames Video Games for Newtown ...
https://mic.com/.../adam-lanza-shooting-fox-news-blames-video-games-for-newtown-... ▾
Fox News, and even Obama adviser David Axelrod, are raising flags on "**violent video games**" in the wake of the Sandy Hook Elementary massacre. Here's why ...

Bill would up taxes on violent video games | WPMT FOX43
https://fox43.com/2019/02/12/bill-would-up-taxes-on-violent-video-games/ ▾
Feb 12, 2019 - Would you pay an extra ten percent for your favorite **video game**? "10 percent tax? ... It's a **new** bill aiming to curb **violence** amongst students...

not always that simple. There are many ways in which a source's content can be relevant. A source may provide

- background information
- key definitions
- support for your idea, through examples, opinions, data, and so on
- an opposing viewpoint that you want to address

A source can also help you further develop an idea of someone else's, introduce a new way of thinking about the subject, and redefine the terms of the discussion.

Let's take a look at another example. The excerpts below are from a student who is writing about the relation between reading fiction and becoming more empathetic (that is, increasing one's ability to understand and share feelings with someone else). The student is arguing that schools should assign more fiction reading so that students can become more empathetic human beings. Notice how she explains the relevance of the sources she has located with her narrow search. Describing one source, she writes the following:

> Because this source reviews three studies that use the technology fMRI (a functional MRI that shows brain activity) to track the parts of the brain that light up when people read fiction, this source could be used to describe from a scientific perspective how reading fiction affects the brain. This is relevant because it will support my claim that reading fiction does affect the brain and makes people more empathetic, capable of feeling emotions similar to those felt by characters they are reading about.

Of another source she writes:

> I could use this piece to define a lot of the terms in my essay. This article explains how terms like *literature*, *fiction*, and *empathy* are defined in scientific studies so it is relevant to the background information I need to give in my essay before I can move on and actually explore the topic.

About a third source she writes:

> This source challenges the idea that reading fiction and empathizing with fictional characters can actually make someone more empathetic toward real people in real life. It is relevant to my essay because it raises questions about different issues that come up when thinking about both empathy and the reading of fiction. Plus, because it challenges my claim, it makes points not made by the other sources that support my claim. For example, it describes the difficulty of determining whether someone is empathetic, let alone more empathetic or less empathetic after reading fiction. It also questions how fiction is defined in these studies. These are important questions because addressing them in my essay will allow me to offer a lot of different perspectives on the topic, which will make it more complex and allow me to respond to these challenges to my argument, which will help me refine my ideas.

As you find sources, take the time to think about and keep track of their potential relevance to your project by asking yourself the following: What will each source contribute? How and why does that contribution matter to my project?

⚙ TRY IT

1. Contemplate your role in source-driven writing.

As you are reminded in this chapter, Burke's description of the parlor can be used as a metaphor for thinking about the types of conversations that take place in academic writing and online. Review that excerpt at the beginning of this chapter and write a paragraph about how Burke's description can help you imagine your role in locating sources and participating in a scholarly conversation.

2. Understand relevance.

List three ways a source may be relevant to a research project. Why is the relevance of your sources important to the process of conducting research and composing source-based projects?

3. Recognize the value of inclusive search and citation practices.

How can seeking out sources written by historically marginalized groups enrich your source-based projects?

4. Practice documenting a broad search.

The chapter you just read discusses the importance of narrowing your searches as necessary. You will recall that broad searches help you get a sense of the larger conversation surrounding your subject matter. This exercise requires that you have a topic you want to research. Once you have chosen a topic or been assigned one, locate five sources through a broad search. Then write a paragraph about each containing the following information to help you consider the relevance of the source to your topic. Each paragraph should include one to two sentences that

- describe the author's expertise or background
- summarize the source, including any conclusions it comes to
- explain the purpose of the piece
- evaluate its relevance for your topic
- identify the intended audience (e.g., the general public, subject specialists, college students)

Below is a sample paragraph.

Brian O'Connell, the author of "Lyft vs. Uber: Which Is Best for Riders and Drivers in 2018?," is a freelance journalist whose work has appeared in some of the top business publications. He is also a former Wall Street bond trader and an author of two books about investing. The point of this article is to explain the subtle but important differences between Lyft and Uber so that readers can make informed decisions about which ride-sharing company is best for them, whether they are looking to work for one of the companies or simply use their services. O'Connell reviews the different geographical regions that each company serves and then discusses other differences that would be of interest to riders, including price differences and the various services that each company offers. For potential drivers, O'Connell reviews how drivers can better get to know each company, which includes taking many rides with each company and asking the drivers directly about their experiences. Ultimately, O'Connell's purpose is to provide a resource for potential ride-sharing customers and drivers who are interested in understanding the differences between the two companies. He concludes that the choice is really a personal one and comes down to individuals' specific priorities. O'Connell's casual and direct style suggests that the piece is intended for a popular audience. This article is potentially useful if I end up needing to compare the two companies in my essay. However, I would need to see if the information in the article and the comparisons O'Connell makes are still current.

5. Practice narrowing online searches.

In this chapter you learned about the importance of making your search terms specific enough to find information directly relevant to your subject and to refine your topic to a manageable scope. Begin a search with the following two terms:

art

literature

How do the results you find help you imagine ways to narrow each term? Create a list of more narrow terms that emerge and might stand in for the broader term "art" and do the same for the term "literature." See how specific you can make each one. An example has been completed for you using the search terms "school" and "technology" (fig. 4.7): notice how the subject is ultimately narrowed down to the uses of literature-based applications on iPads in Advanced Placement literature courses.

Fig. 4.7. Example of ways to narrow the search terms "school" and "technology"

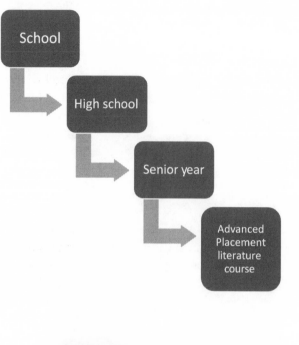

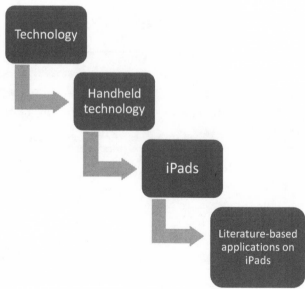

5

Go to the
(Primary) Source!

RELATED APPENDIX ACTIVITIES: 1.3, 2.1, 3.2, 3.3

Understanding the difference between primary and secondary sources will help you better evaluate sources, including those found on the World Wide Web. Whether you are looking for the most accurate account of an event that interests you for personal reasons or sources that will be of use to you in an academic research project, this chapter teaches you how to identify primary sources and encourages you to use them whenever possible so that you are not dependent on others' interpretations of sources.

What Are Primary and Secondary Sources?

Primary sources provide firsthand, or direct, information. Examples of primary sources include photographs, video and audio recordings, letters, diaries, government and legal documents, speeches, historical documents and artifacts, and interviews. Artistic creations are also primary sources. In literary studies, primary sources also include literature. In the sciences, research studies and reports are also primary sources. Although not always considered appropriate sources to use within academic settings, social media posts, such as tweets and *TikTok* videos, also qualify as primary sources.

Secondary sources are created after and as a result of primary sources. They offer secondary accounts of the information or evidence given in primary sources. Secondary sources, in other words, are *about* primary sources. They summarize, interpret, or draw on primary sources in some way. For example, a newspaper article about Anne Frank's diary is a secondary source, a scholarly article about Jane Austen's novel *Pride and Prejudice* is a secondary source, and a review of a Broadway play is a secondary source. While secondary sources are important because they offer different perspectives on a subject, going to the primary source allows you to form your own judgments, interpretations, and conclusions without being swayed by what others think.

The distinction between primary and secondary sources, though, is not always cut-and-dried. For example, a newspaper or magazine article about a viral video is a secondary source, whereas the viral video is the primary source. But a newspaper or magazine article can also be a primary source. An article about an event that just took place, particularly if the writer was on the scene of that event or interviewed witnesses, is a primary source. In other words, it is the content of the source—as opposed to its format—that helps you determine whether it is a primary or secondary source.

To determine if a source is a primary source, ask yourself the following questions about its author:

- What is the author's connection to the information written?
- If the author is recounting an event, was the author there?
- Did the author read about or hear about the event or subject from another source?

If the author is describing something they witnessed firsthand, then you are working with a primary source. But if the author refers to other sources or describes the experiences of others, then you are dealing with a secondary source. The following databases contain primary sources:

The American Civil War: Letters and Diaries

American Periodicals Series

Digital National Security Archive

Early English Books Online

North American Women's Letters and Diaries

Perseus Digital Library

ProQuest Historical Newspapers

ProQuest Statistical Abstract of the United States

Queen Victoria's Journals

Trench Journals and Unit Magazines of the First World War

Visual History Archive

Vogue Archive

Women Writers Project

As you look over the list of databases above, notice why they contain primary sources. These are not databases full of articles or essays *about* civil war letters or diaries *about* early English books. Instead, all these databases contain original, or primary, sources—the very letters and diaries themselves.

If you are searching the World Wide Web and not databases, finding primary sources can be more difficult. This is because the web is flush with secondary sources that appear alongside primary sources. Fortunately, though, the very nature of the web often allows you to find a link to the primary source. Let's look at the example in figure 5.1. The article from the Animals section of *Simplemost* (www.simplemost.com) is a secondary

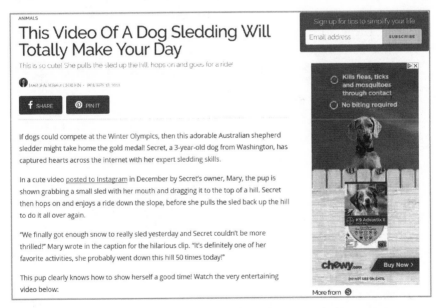

Fig. 5.1. Secondary source containing a link to the original video, a primary source

source because it is *about* the video of a dog sledding. But notice that there is a link to the video itself, the primary source, which is posted on *Instagram*. You can (and should!) follow that direct path to the primary source. As the researcher, it is your responsibility to compile the most accurate information available. Often, as in the case of the video of the dog sledding, compiling the most accurate information involves seeking out primary sources whenever they are available. Working your way back from secondary sources to primary sources, which often involves moving among a variety of sites and platforms, will help you assemble credible information.

Distinguishing between primary and secondary sources is crucial to becoming digitally literate because it means that you understand that secondary sources are filtering an event or subject through someone else's perspective. Only when you locate and engage with primary sources—before turning to secondary sources if you need to—can you determine for yourself what the sources mean. Otherwise, you are left dealing with secondary sources that have their own biases. For example, notice how the secondary sources shown in figures 5.2 and 5.3 describe the post that Mark Zuckerberg, the founder and leader of Meta (the parent organization of the platforms *Facebook*, *Instagram*, and *WhatsApp*), wrote about *Facebook*'s role in the 2016 election. In the first piece, by Kathleen Chaykowski, Zuckerberg and *Facebook* are described in rather negative terms (fig. 5.2). Chaykowski points out that while Zuckerberg did apologize, he also used the opportunity to continue to defend *Facebook*. She opens the article with some skepticism about his apology: "But that dose of contrition came mixed with a spirited defense of Facebook and its role in the election. . . . [He] forcefully made the case that Facebook was ultimately a force for social good by enabling discussion of key political issues, despite a small number of problematic ads." Chaykowski could have opened her article in any manner, but this approach paints Zuckerberg in an unflattering light by suggesting that he used the apology to downplay *Facebook*'s role in the election's outcome and to highlight *Facebook*'s positive contributions instead.

Mike Murphy, the author of the second piece, makes different choices (fig. 5.3). He notes that Zuckerberg "admitted he underestimated the impact of fake news on his social network," which paints Zuckerberg as

Zuckerberg Defends Facebook's Role In Election But 'Regrets' Dismissing Impact Of Fake News

Kathleen Chaykowski Forbes Staff

f

y

in

But that dose of contrition came mixed with a spirited defense of Facebook and its role in the election. In a response to the critical tweet from Trump, he forcefully made the case that Facebook was ultimately a force for social good by enabling discussion of key political issues, despite a small number of problematic ads.

"After the election, I made a comment that I thought the idea misinformation on Facebook changed the outcome of the election was a crazy idea," Zuckerberg said in his post. "Calling that crazy was dismissive and I regret it. This is too important an issue to be dismissive."

Zuckerberg made his remarks in a Facebook post on Thursday, responding to Trump's tweet, which accused Facebook, along with television networks, *The New York Times* and the *Washington Post*, of being "anti-Trump."

"Trump says Facebook is against him," Zuckerberg wrote. "Liberals say we helped Trump. Both sides are upset about ideas and content they don't like. That's what running a platform for all ideas looks like."

Fig. 5.2. Secondary source that takes a negative spin on the subject of a primary source

someone willing to acknowledge mistakes. While both Murphy and Chaykowski give voice to Zuckerberg's comments that he can't help upsetting both sides—those who say *Facebook* affected the 2016 presidential election and helped Trump win and those who say *Facebook* is anti-Trump—Chaykowski's readers may come away less sympathetic to Zuckerberg because of the way her article seems to question the sincerity of Zuckerberg's apology. Like Chaykowski, Murphy made choices about how he was going to present *Facebook*, Zuckerberg, and the situation. The two pieces use some of the same information very differently,

Fig. 5.3. Secondary source that portrays the subject of the primary source more favorably

SHARE   COMMENTS 74   Aa

Facebook Chief Executive Mark Zuckerberg admitted he underestimated the impact of fake news on his social network during last year's election, as another divisive Russian-backed ad buy came to light.

> *"After the election, I made a comment that I thought the idea misinformation on Facebook changed the outcome of the election was a crazy idea. Calling that crazy was dismissive and I regret it. This is too important an issue to be dismissive."*
>
> Mark Zuckerberg

Zuckerberg made his comments in a **Facebook post Wednesday** in response to a **tweet by President Donald Trump** earlier in the day claiming that Facebook was "anti-Trump."

"Trump says Facebook is against him. Liberals say we helped Trump. Both sides are upset about ideas and content they don't like. That's what running a platform for all ideas looks like," Zuckerberg said, noting that Facebook spread political messages from both sides and that its "get out the vote" effort helped more than 2 million people to register to vote.

Last week, Facebook **FB, -0.28%** turned over about 3,000 Russia-linked ads to government investigators looking into Russian meddling in the 2016 presidential race, and announced **new transparency measures for political ads.**

Later Wednesday, CNN reported that at least **one of the Russian-bought ads referenced Black Lives Matter** and was targeted at audiences in Ferguson, Mo., and Baltimore, the sites of large protests following the deaths of black men at the hands of police.

though. Chaykowski's piece seems biased against Zuckerberg and *Facebook,* while Murphy offers a more generous reading of the situation and a positive portrayal of Zuckerberg.

You could trust what one or the other of these secondary sources says about the letter, but why do that when you can locate and interpret the letter yourself? The excerpt in figure 5.4 is the primary source to which both of these secondary sources refer—Zuckerberg's letter. The letter itself, which is a *Facebook* post, provides direct access to Zuckerberg's words without the bias that may come from others who are describing, summarizing, and interpreting the letter. Part of being digitally literate involves tracking down primary sources to ensure you have the opportunity to make up your own mind about the source before others (i.e., secondary sources) influence what you think.

I Found the Primary Source—Now What?

Once you have found your primary source, you will need to understand what it says. This section gives you reading strategies and some online tools to help you keep track of and understand primary sources.*

Digital Tools for Keeping Track of Primary (and Other) Sources

Before you can engage and work with primary and other sources, you need to have a system for keeping your sources organized as you move through the research process. Research management platforms like *NoodleTools* and reference management systems like *EasyBib, Evernote,* and *RefWorks* can be helpful as you locate and save primary sources. Research management platforms help you stay organized because they provide a space in which you can generate citations for your sources, archive your sources, annotate them, take other kinds of notes, outline and draft, and even collaborate with others. Reference management systems allow you to store all your sources in one space and help you generate citations for each one.

---

*Some of the descriptions of the reading strategies in this section also appear in chapter 2 of *A Writer's Guide to Mindful Reading,* WAC Clearinghouse / University Press of Colorado, © 2017 by Ellen C. Carillo under a Creative Commons Attribution-NonCommercial-NoDerivatives 4.0 International License. Used with permission.

Fig. 5.4. The primary source described by the secondary sources in figures 5.2 and 5.3

 Mark Zuckerberg
September 27, 2017 · Palo Alto, CA ·

I want to respond to President Trump's tweet this morning claiming Facebook has always been against him.

Every day I work to bring people together and build a community for everyone. We hope to give all people a voice and create a platform for all ideas.

Trump says Facebook is against him. Liberals say we helped Trump. Both sides are upset about ideas and content they don't like. That's what running a platform for all ideas looks like.

The facts suggest the greatest role Facebook played in the 2016 election was different from what most are saying:

- More people had a voice in this election than ever before. There were billions of interactions discussing the issues that may have never happened offline. Every topic was discussed, not just what the media covered.

- This was the first US election where the internet was a primary way candidates communicated. Every candidate had a Facebook page to communicate directly with tens of millions of followers every day.

- Campaigns spent hundreds of millions advertising online to get their messages out even further. That's 1000x more than any problematic ads we've found.

- We ran "get out the vote" efforts that helped as many as 2 million people register to vote. To put that in perspective, that's bigger than the get out the vote efforts of the Trump and Clinton campaigns put together. That's a big deal.

After the election, I made a comment that I thought the idea misinformation on Facebook changed the outcome of the election was a crazy idea. Calling that crazy was dismissive and I regret it. This is too important an issue to be dismissive. But the data we have has always shown that our broader impact -- from giving people a voice to enabling candidates to communicate directly to helping millions of people vote -- played a far bigger role in this election.

We will continue to work to build a community for all people. We will do our part to defend against nation states attempting to spread misinformation and subvert elections. We'll keep working to ensure the integrity of free and fair elections around the world, and to ensure our community is a platform for all ideas and force for good in democracy.

 274K   18K Comments   15K Shares

 Share

There are many other digital tools that can support and enhance your academic work. The next section includes strategies for reading texts, many of which are accompanied by a short discussion of specific digital tools that can support these strategies.

Strategies for Reading Texts

Five reading strategies—annotating, reading rhetorically, reading aloud to paraphrase, mapping, and summarizing—will help you understand text-based primary sources.

Annotating

You have probably been asked by instructors to mark up something you are reading. Maybe you have been asked to jot down questions or notes in the margins, highlight the important parts, or circle words you don't know. Maybe you have developed these habits on your own. The act of marking up a text is commonly referred to as *annotating*. The word *annotate* comes from the Latin word for "to note or mark," or "to note down." To annotate is exactly that: it's when you make notes on a text based on what you are thinking as you read that text.

When you annotate, you are writing as you read. You make notes, comment, react, and raise questions in the margins of your text. Your annotations can serve as the basis for the more extensive contributions you will be expected to make in formal assignments and essays. For example, if you need to write an essay about something you have read, you can return to your annotations—to the questions you posed and comments you made in the margins—because these are moments in which you were already interacting with the text and its author. You can then develop your preliminary interactions into a more detailed and comprehensive response.

Annotations can be handwritten on a printed text or applied digitally on an electronic text using annotation management systems like *Diigo, iAnnotate, Hypothes.is, Perusall,* and *Epic Pen.* These annotation software programs allow you to mark up web pages (and other digital documents), but other programs exist with more limited applications. For example, if you are reading a PDF, you can also use the comment bubbles in *Adobe Acrobat* to annotate the document. Figure 5.5 shows an example of a text annotated by a student. Notice that the student uses annotations to ask questions, summarize ideas, challenge points, and make personal connections.

READING RHETORICALLY

Rhetoric refers to the means of persuasion at a writer's disposal. When you read something rhetorically you are paying attention to how certain elements of the text influence you as you read. By paying attention to them, you become aware of how a text makes its ideas understandable to you. This awareness, in turn, can help you make choices about how to make your ideas understandable and persuasive to those who read your writing.

When reading rhetorically, there are at least five rhetorical elements to which you should pay attention: purpose, audience, claims, evidence, and design. Ask yourself the following questions:

- What is the author's purpose for writing? Is the author arguing a point? Bringing awareness to a problem? Trying to make sense of an experience? Calling people to action?
- Who is the intended audience? To whom does the author seem to be writing?
- What claims does the author make or allude to?
- What kinds of evidence are used (e.g., does the author rely on scientific data, anecdotes, personal experience)?
- How does the design reflect the content? To what extent does it contribute to the goals of the piece of writing?

Additionally, there are three specific types of appeals that writers might make to persuade readers:

- Ethos—appeals to credibility. Notice how the author tries to persuade readers by establishing credibility.
- Logos—appeals to logic. Notice how the author uses the logic of arguments or claims to persuade readers.
- Pathos—appeals to emotions. Notice how the author tries to persuade readers by engaging their emotions.

Fig. 5.5. An annotated text

Since the 1950s we have been hearing that Johnny can't read. In 1975, *Newsweek* informed us that Johnny can't write, either. Over the years, a range of reasons for Johnny's illiteracy have been offered. Most recently, technology has been named one of the culprits. Johnny spends too much time on the computer and not enough time reading books. He spends so much time texting and tweeting that he has forgotten how to write correctly, how to spell, how to develop ideas in more than 140 characters. Public outcries about literacy (or lack thereof) often lead to a closer look at the education system. The public raises questions surrounding why colleges and universities in particular—where Johnny would be expected to gain in-depth and comprehensive literacy skills— are not doing a better job. What is often neglected in these public debates about the best way to teach literacy at the college level is that reading and writing are connected practices and, as such, the best way to teach them is together. It is a bad idea to continue privileging writing at the expense of reading.

This problematic separation of the connected practices of reading and writing is no longer an issue in students' early schooling, where they are taught reading and writing simultaneously. Although it took decades for elementary school teachers and curricula developers to realize that young children need not learn how to read before they learned how to write, language arts instructors now teach reading and writing alongside each other. They do so because research has shown that students learn to read and write better when they are instructed in both simultaneously. This research, for example, shows that students' phonic skills are reinforced when children practice both reading and writing the same

Johnny stands in for all students.

Reasons why Johnny isn't a good reader or writer.

Reading isn't taught as much as writing in college. (But shouldn't college students know how to read?)

Young students are taught reading and writing at the same time.

About What Good Writing Is   39

words. As they get a little older, students begin to develop an awareness of genres or types of text, which, like the study of phonics, is also further reinforced by a concurrent focus on reading and writing. As students read (or are read to) they learn to recognize typical elements of fiction, which they then imitate in their own writing and stories. Even a two-year-old who has been read to consistently will recognize that "once upon a time" indicates the beginning of a story, and will often begin that same way when asked to make up his or her own.

By the time students arrive in college, stories beginning with "once upon a time" are long gone, and in their place are difficult and dense texts—often multimedia texts— from a range of fields each with its own set of conventions. Instead of drawing on models of early literacy education that focus on teaching reading and writing simultaneously, college and universities largely privilege writing over reading. This hierarchy is evidenced by the universal first-year writing requirement in American colleges and universities, as well as by writing across the curriculum programs. The integrated approach to teaching reading and writing falls away to students' peril and causes great frustration in the professors who often attribute students' struggles in their courses to poor writing ability, when these problems are often related to students' reading difficulties. While students' eyes may make their way over every word, that does not mean that students have comprehended a text or that they are prepared to successfully complete the writing tasks associated with the reading, which often involve summary, analysis,

I agree—reading in college is hard.

In First-Year Composition we didn't talk about reading.

This is about a specific kind of reading. It's not that college students can't read but that they can't read difficult texts in these complex ways.

The ability to recognize these three appeals as you read complements other abilities this guide seeks to hone. For example, judging the author's ethos, or credibility, enables you to assess whether the author has the expertise to engage with the subject. Being able to recognize the logic (logos) or lack thereof in a piece of writing is important as you determine if what you are reading is credible. Finally, if you recognize that an author is appealing to your emotions through pathos, you can become more aware of the role your emotions may be playing in how you are evaluating the author's position.

READING ALOUD TO PARAPHRASE

This strategy really consists of two individual strategies combined into one—reading aloud and paraphrasing. Feel free to separate them if that works better for you. For example, if you are in a location where it is not appropriate to read aloud or if you are deaf or hard of hearing, you can simply paraphrase what you are reading, which on its own is an important strategy to practice. The combination, though, brings together complementary approaches to reading: reading aloud highlights each word as you hear it, and paraphrasing requires that you not only hear all the words but also translate them into your own words. This reading approach, then, fosters concentration in ways that some others may not, and it may be especially helpful when you are faced with particularly difficult sections of a text. If you prefer to be read to, many smartphones will read aloud to you, and there is text-to-speech software you can download to do the same if you prefer. As you read aloud to paraphrase or as you listen to a text, you need not paraphrase every single word, but you should stop every few sentences or so and annotate the text by writing, in your own words, about what you just read or heard.

MAPPING

Mapping is a visual tool that can help you organize and understand what you are reading. When you map a text, you present visually what the text says. You might map the whole text, a few pages, or a single element (such as a text's argument). When you map a text, you become highly aware of the relations among its different parts, and the visual representation often highlights aspects of the text that aren't otherwise visible. Maps come in different shapes and sizes and can be adjusted to suit your needs. Perhaps the most common is the web (or radial) map, in which the main idea is in the center and threads radiate from it to less central ideas. From those threads come other threads and so on from there.

Maps can be developed by hand or with software. *MindMeister*, *ClickUp*, and *Lucidchart* offer digital tools for mapping, as do *Creately* and *Cmap*. There are also graphic organizer templates available on *Thinkport* that can be downloaded in *Microsoft Word* or as PDFs. The most important element of any map is that it allows you to see how different elements of a text are related. Maps may also help you understand the relations among concepts or ideas discussed in a text. Often, these visual representations allow you to recognize relations you hadn't noticed while reading. For example, figure 5.6 can help you visualize the relation between the Internet and the web as it might be laid out in an article about technology. As discussed in chapter 3, the Internet and the web are not the same thing even though we often use the terms interchangeably. The web is merely one of the services that the Internet offers. While an article on the difference between the web and the Internet may be hard to understand, creating a visual of what that article says can help clarify the concepts in the article. This map makes it clear that the web is just one among many of the services offered by the Internet and, therefore, is not synonymous with the Internet.

Summarizing

The goal of summarizing is to boil down an entire source to its main ideas. This strategy depends, in part, on your successful completion of the strategies listed above. After determining a source's main ideas and details by applying the above strategies, summarizing them using a limited number of words—say, twenty-five or fifty—forces you to make decisions about the source's most important elements and how they relate to one another.

Strategies for Visual Sources

The primary source you locate may be a *YouTube* video, a film, a graphic or comic, a photograph, a drawing, a painting, a map, a sculpture, or

Fig. 5.6. Map showing the relation between the Internet and the World Wide Web

something else that does not rely on text to help create its meaning. The three strategies below—analyzing rhetorically (which you'll recognize from the list above), listing your observations, and considering context—will help you better understand what you are seeing when the primary source has no text. With technology-focused journalists like Farhad Manjoo predicting a post-text future wherein images and other visuals we encounter daily exceed the amount of text (or writing) we encounter, these strategies may become that much more important in the coming years.

ANALYZING RHETORICALLY

The principles of rhetorical reading, detailed above, remain relevant when comprehending visual texts, too. For visual sources, though, the activity you are engaging in is called *rhetorical analysis* because it refers to sources that contain limited text or no text at all. Paying attention to the rhetorical elements of purpose, audience, claims, evidence, and design will help you develop a rhetorical analysis of visual sources. For example, just as you would consider the author's purpose for writing an article, you would consider a person's purpose for creating a video and uploading it online. Here are the five rhetorical elements from earlier in the chapter, slightly revised so they apply to visual texts:

Purpose. What is the purpose of the visual source? Is its creator arguing a point? Bringing awareness to a problem? Trying to make sense of an experience? Calling people to action?

Audience. For whom is the visual source intended?

Claims. What kinds of claims does the visual source make?

Evidence. What kinds of evidence are used in the visual source?

Design. How does the design of the visual source contribute to its meaning?

Just as you do for alphabetic texts, you may consider the different kinds of appeals that visual sources make:

Ethos. Notice how the visual source tries to persuade readers by establishing its credibility.

Logos. Notice how the visual source uses logic to persuade readers.

Pathos. Notice how the visual source tries to persuade readers by engaging their emotions.

Additional considerations when working with visual sources include paying attention to how the various design elements of the visual source contribute to its meaning. For example, you can consider the source's use of images, color, graphics, layout, typeface or font, arrangement, and scale. All these elements affect how a visual source influences its audience.

Visual sources may also take the shape of charts, graphs, infographics, and tables, which are collectively called *data visualizations* because they represent data in a visual manner. Data visualizations have been shown to be highly persuasive. As such, it is important to pay attention to how data visualizations are presenting data instead of simply assuming their veracity, as studies show we are prone to do: for example, a series of studies conducted on the effect of advertisements for new medications corroborates this notion (Tal). In the study, some participants were presented with both written information and a graph about the medication while others were just given the written information. The perceived effectiveness of the medication increased twenty-three percent when the graph accompanied the information. In a related study, nearly ninety-seven percent of participants who saw the graph believed the medication would reduce illness, while nearly sixty-seven percent of participants who did not see the graph thought so. In these cases, the graphs were very basic and presented no new information, thereby corroborating researchers' consistent findings that graphs, charts, and tables have an air of objectivity about them and appear scientific in ways that other forms of presenting information do not. Whether or not we realize it, we value data visualizations and are more likely to believe information presented in this way. To better understand data visualizations, you can analyze them rhetorically, similarly to how you would analyze other visual sources, as described just above. However, when analyzing data visualizations, it's best to focus on three of the five rhetorical elements:

> **Purpose**. What is the purpose of the data visualization? Is it meant to inform, educate, or persuade you?
>
> **Audience**. For whom is the visual source intended?
>
> **Design**. How does the design of the visual source contribute to its meaning?

Using the bar graph in figure 5.7 as an example, we might answer the above questions in the following way:

> The purpose of the visualization is to inform those interested in the ages of *TikTok* users in the United States and show the comparison among users by age group.
>
> The audience is people who want statistics about social media users by age.

Bar graphs make it easy to compare sets of data between different groups. In this case, the graph helps readers quickly recognize and compare the use of *TikTok* among different age groups. The simple design of the bar graph, which includes just two axes, makes the comparison especially visible. This would not be the case with a different kind of data visualization, such as a pie chart, which is used to compare parts of a whole.

Because of the documented persuasive powers of charts and graphs, it's important to also have the tools for evaluating the credibility of data visualizations. If we look at the bar graph on *TikTok* users in the United States, we can assess its credibility in a few ways. First, as you can see, it is accompanied by source information. Clicking the hyperlinks to the right of the graph would allow you to read about the organization that collected the data and other relevant information. To further corroborate the credibility of the graph, you can use lateral reading, a strategy explained in the next chapter, wherein you move away from the graph itself and use other sources on the web to learn more about the organization that collected the data, which will help you determine the credibility of the graph. You can also read laterally by going to other sites on the web to see if the data in this graph resemble data collected on the same subject by other organizations.

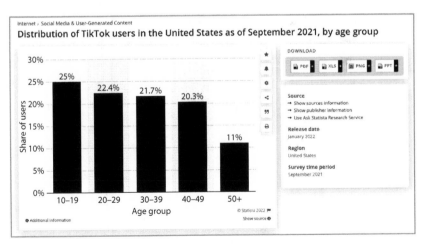

Fig. 5.7. Example of a bar graph, a type of data visualization

Listing Your Observations

Like the mapping strategy described above, this one involves re-presenting the source. Listing everything you notice about a visual source can reveal connections you may have missed. The act of writing while you deliberately observe the source can also spark new ideas about it.

Considering Context

Understanding the context of the visual source allows you to interpret a lot about it. To reconstruct the context, you can ask yourself a series of investigative questions, beginning with Who? What? Where? When? and Why? For example, you might ask, Who took this photograph? When was it taken? Why was it taken? Answering these and related questions will help you construct some background, which will help you understand the source. You might be able to answer some of these questions by observing the source itself. If the visual source does not provide this information, you can always conduct a reverse image search (described in chapter 9) or consider other secondary sources that may provide information and context that help you determine, for example, why and when a photograph was taken.

Strategies for Audio Sources

If you locate an audio primary source, you will need to listen to it rather than read or view it. Examples of audio primary sources include recorded interviews, speeches, performances, and podcasts. Asking yourself the following questions, many of which overlap with the rhetorical-analysis approach discussed above, will help you make sense of audio primary sources:

- What type of recording is it (e.g., speech, interview, podcast)?
- Who contributed to it (e.g., who is featured in it, who produced it, who broadcasted it)?
- When was it made?
- Where was it made?
- Can you infer the purpose for its creation?

- Based on its content, who seems to be the intended audience for the recording?
- If there is music on the recording, what does it contribute?
- Do you learn anything from this audio source that you did not know before listening to it or that hasn't surfaced in other sources you may be using?

Figuring out what kind of recording you are listening to is the first step to understanding the source. For example, if you are listening to an interview you will want to ask questions about both participants—the interviewer and interviewee—to better understand the audio source, including its purpose. You would need to consider who is conducting the interview and how that informs its purpose and audience.

Considering who contributed to the recording is important for understanding its context. Contributors to a recording include anyone who speaks, sings, or makes other utterances on it as well as the person, group, or company that published it. Once you know who has contributed to the recording, you can seek out secondary sources that provide more information about the contributors, including biographical details like where they worked when the recording was made. Such information might even help you piece together why the recording was made and reveal any potential biases that may inflect the source.

It is also important to imagine the audience for whom the recording was created. Doing so further adds to the context for the source. One way to determine the intended audience is to consider what knowledge about the subject the recording assumes the audience already has. For example, does the recording explain any concepts or provide information about people it mentions, or does it assume that listeners do not need these explanations?

Primary audio sources may not include explanations or information at all—for example, they may be composed solely of music. When analyzing an audio source composed only of music, you can ask yourself the questions listed above, but you might also consider how the music makes you feel. Do you think the music is intended to evoke specific emotions in you, such as happiness or sadness?

Some audio sources, such as podcasts, will use music alongside speech to set the tone, underscore important points, and evoke emotions in its listeners. Understanding the role of the music in such an audio source will help you understand the source as a whole. Keep in mind that music may be used in different ways throughout the source: music in the introduction may be used to set the tone while music may be used throughout the recording to highlight important moments, inspire emotional responses in listeners, or mark the movement from one segment of the recording to another. Music may be used at the end of a recording to let listeners know they have reached the end.

Can't Find the Primary Source?

So far this chapter has assumed that you can find all the primary sources you need, but that may not always be the case. If you can't find a primary source, the best way to proceed is to apply what you learn in this book (especially in chapters 6–9) about how to read across the web, which will help you determine a source's credibility, relevance to your project, and context.

✿ TRY IT

1. Practice finding primary sources.

Choose a subject and conduct an online search to find at least one primary source related to that subject. Then, write a few sentences about the characteristics that make it a primary source.

2. Practice distinguishing primary sources from secondary sources.

Review the following list of sources and determine which are primary sources and which are secondary sources:

- history textbook
- Declaration of Independence
- movie review

- op-ed about a country's health-care program
- government documents outlining a country's health-care program
- transcript from a court case
- tweet written by an individual describing an event
- retweet
- article about the United States Constitution on a credible website about American history
- United States Constitution

3. Practice rhetorical reading.

Return to the reading at the end of chapter 2 and read it rhetorically. Referring to the section on reading rhetorically in this chapter, select one example of the source's appeal to each of the three rhetorical techniques: credibility (ethos), logic (logos), and emotion (pathos). Also indicate which appeal seems most common.

4. Compose a rhetorical analysis of a visual source.

Choose a visual source—such as a *YouTube* video, film, graphic or comic, photograph, drawing, painting, map, or something else that does not rely on text to help create its meaning—and compose a rhetorical analysis of the source. Use the questions in the section "Analyzing Rhetorically" above in this chapter to guide your analysis. Also, select one example of the source's appeal to each of the three rhetorical techniques: credibility (ethos), logic (logos), and emotion (pathos).

5. Practice writing a twenty-five-word summary.

Return to the reading at the end of chapter 2 and compose a twenty-five-word summary of it. Then write about how you chose what to include in that summary and what to omit. In this reflection, be sure to offer a detailed account of your composing process. Did you begin with a summary longer than twenty-five words and cut from there? Did you begin with a summary under twenty-five words and expand from there? Explain your process.

6

Surveying the Conversation by Reading Laterally

RELATED APPENDIX ACTIVITIES: 1.2, 3.2, 3.3

This book uses conversation as a metaphor both for searching the World Wide Web and for conducting research projects generally. Remember that to make contributions to a conversation by building on what others have said, first you must listen. Why? Because building on what others have said requires that you understand the relation among individual contributions and the merit of each one. And it's usually not possible to immediately and accurately judge a person's contribution to a conversation as true or false, right or wrong, credible or not credible. The same is true with research materials: they cannot be assessed in isolation but must be put in conversation with one another. Thinking about research as an act of listening will help you put sources in conversation as you read them and, ultimately, help you determine the credibility of sources. In fact, this way of reading—called *lateral reading*—is how professional fact-checkers assess sources (Wineburg and McGrew).

What Is Reading Laterally?

Reading laterally means reading *across* the web. Educators Sam Wineburg and Sarah McGrew, who first used the term *lateral* to describe this method of reading, characterize the approach as follows: "When reading laterally, one leaves a website and opens new tabs along a horizontal axis in order to use the resources of the Internet to learn more about a site and its claims." They compare lateral reading to *vertical reading*, or reading up and down: "Lateral reading contrasts with vertical reading. Reading vertically, our eyes go up and down a screen to evaluate the features of a site. Does it look professional, free of typos and banner ads? Does it quote well-known sources? Are bias or faulty logic detectable?" Wineburg and McGrew found in their study that the lateral readers who "paid little attention to such features, leaping off a site after a few seconds and opening new tabs" were more successful than those who read vertically. Lateral readers more efficiently and effectively analyzed the credibility of the sites put before them because they "investigated a site by leaving it" (38). Those participants who remained tethered to a single website—instead of moving outward to others—were not as efficient or effective in their assessments. Focusing exclusively on a site to determine its credibility is not enough. Even a well-designed and grammatically correct website can be untrustworthy.

You might also think of lateral reading as cross-referencing, a term you may be more familiar with. When you cross-reference something, you are verifying information found in one source by checking to see if it can be located in other sources. Keep in mind, though, that some websites reuse information from other sites. If the information is copied verbatim (that is, word for word) from another site, that is a sign that the information may not have been verified. You should continue looking to other sites to verify the material. To verify information found on a website or to judge the likely quality of the information provided, check to see whether other sites contain the same information as well as what they say about the site, its subject, its publisher, its author, and other elements. You do not need to read every related website for its content. You should, however, move purposefully from one site to the next. Doing so will allow you to piece together how the source fits within the larger conversation. Once you do that, you can begin to evaluate the source and its credibility.

Lateral and Vertical Reading Compared

Let's consider an example of how lateral and vertical reading differ. Figure 6.1 shows a screenshot of the home page of *Natural News* (www.naturalnews.com). The site is designed to provide news and information about leading a naturally healthy lifestyle. If we apply the CRAAP test (described in chapter 1) and consider the site's currency, relevance, authority, accuracy, and purpose, *Natural News* passes! The information is current: articles have been written within the last twenty-four hours. If you are working on a project about leading a natural lifestyle, the information on the website is certainly relevant; its tabs contain a range of sources about natural foods, including blogs, reports, news articles, and infographics from both scholarly and popular sources, which could be useful depending on the requirements of your assignment. As for authority, each article on the home page of the site is credited to an author. You can even click on each author's name to be taken to other articles the author has written for *Natural News*, which allows you to evaluate other works by the author and assess the author's expertise. The information on the site is supported by a range of evidence that gives the appearance of accuracy. In figure 6.1, the toolbar at the top of the site's home page includes, among others, the sections Labs, Science, Reference, Reports, and Infographics, which take users to seemingly credible scientific information, websites, data, reports, and even to the *Natural Science Journal*, located at a .org domain. You will also notice that the banner at the top of the page indicates that the website is "the world's top news source on natural health" and is "part of the natural news network." These credentials

Fig. 6.1. Example of vertical reading: *Natural News* website

would seem to add to the accuracy of the site's content. Finally, the purpose of the information seems to be to inform users. While the site is selling natural supplements, most of the site is geared toward educating users about the importance of eating natural foods, avoiding toxins, and other topics related to leading a healthy life. Reading vertically (or down) the source by using the CRAAP test, this site looks to be credible.

Let's see what happens, though, when we move away from the website to which the CRAAP test tethered us. First, we can do a quick *Google* search for "Natural News," the title of the website. The first five results reveal little to suggest that the site is not credible (fig. 6.2). The word *conspiracy* does get mentioned in the *Wikipedia* entry, but we know that *Wikipedia* is not necessarily a credible site. Moreover, the four search results just below the *Wikipedia* link don't suggest anything along those lines. But the sixth result should raise some red flags. It's from *Snopes* (www .snopes.com), the online fact-checking, hoax-busting website.

The search results offer hints that *Natural News* may not be a legitimate news source: the sources generated by *Google* also include an article by *Grist* (grist.org) titled "Don't Believe Anything You Read at Natural News" and an article from *Forbes* (www.forbes.com) called "Natural-Nonsense: Science Supporters Condemn Natural News." When investigating, you would then want to move laterally to these sources, check them out, evaluate *their* credibility, and so on, until you have cross-referenced or verified the information using several sources. And some sites may be messier to evaluate than this one. After all, not all sites will appear on *Snopes*. Even if *Snopes* had not been listed in the results for *Natural News*, the references linked to in the *Wikipedia* entry and the *Grist* and *Forbes* articles would have suggested that the site lacks credibility. The point is that while you could have spent fifteen minutes on the *Natural News* site to determine its credibility, in less than half a second *Google* was able to return results that suggest the website is not credible, thereby encouraging you to explore further.

Keep in mind, though, that recognizing the *Natural News* site lacks credibility required you to read beyond the first few results on the page: it was the sixth result (not including *Wikipedia*), fairly low on that first page of results, that began to suggest the site may not be credible. If you had stopped reading after the first few results or if you were not paying

Fig. 6.2. Example of the first step in reading laterally about *Natural News*

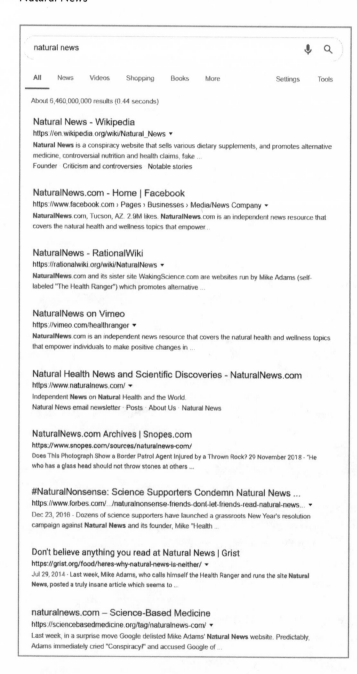

attention to the descriptions below each result, you could have missed an indication that the site is problematic.

Planning Where to Go Next

As they read laterally, the more successful participants in Wineburg and McGrew's study were also committed to "taking bearings," which involves

> mak[ing] a plan for moving forward. Taking bearings is what sailors, aviators, and hikers do to plot their course toward a desired destination. Although correct bearings do not guarantee that travelers will reach that destination, heading in the right direction substantially increases their chances. To take bearings, web searchers obviously don't use a physical compass. But they need metaphorical compasses just as much as hikers need real ones. (37)

Less successful study participants did not take bearings and instead engaged in vertical reading and what Wineburg and McGrew call "fluttering, aimlessly moving across the screen" (28).

To practice taking our bearings, let's use the *Natural News* example. When we plugged "Natural News" into *Google* to begin laterally reading about the site, we noticed that the sixth result and some beyond it raised questions about the credibility of the site. Let's pursue those leads. Taking our bearings includes developing a plan to move forward. To avoid fluttering, we want to keep this plan in mind and move ahead in a purposeful and strategic way. We can first make a list of the sites that suggested to us that *Natural News* may not be credible. The *Google* search returned three such sites (not including *Wikipedia*), which is sufficient in this context because each site discusses *Natural News* in detail. In other cases, you may need one or two more sources, for a total of four or five, to allow you to make a definitive evaluation of the site in question. In the *Natural News* example, the three results that most clearly question the site's credibility are *Snopes*, *Grist*, and *Forbes*.

Let's begin with *Snopes*. You can read about *Natural News* on *Snopes*, but how do you know that *Snopes* is trustworthy? Read laterally! Do a search for "snopes.com" and begin to read what other sites say about its reliability as a source. Continue to do so until you feel confident about whether you can trust *Snopes*. Then review your plan, which is the list of sources you are going to assess.

The next source is *Grist*. Don't be tricked by its address, grist.org. Remember that *.org* does not necessarily mean that the source is credible. Instead, stay on task and take a quick look at the story about *Natural News* that appears on *Grist* before moving outward to see what other sites say about *Grist*, as you did with *Snopes*, until you know that you either have or lack confidence in *Grist* as a source. Next, sticking to your plan, assess *Forbes*. At the end of your journey you should know whether you can trust these three sources, all of which indicate that *Natural News* is not credible.

Understanding Your Biases and Emotional Responses As You Read Laterally

When you read, there is a lot going on in your brain. You are decoding the words and processing their meaning. You are also reacting to what you are reading, and in some cases that reaction will be a strong one. What you are reading might make you experience various emotions, including anger, fear, happiness, and sadness. It is important to be able to gauge your responses to sources because doing so gives you insight into how you feel about a source. If you are going to evaluate a source fairly, you need to understand how your reaction to it might affect that evaluation.

Bias

You are likely familiar with the term *bias*. A bias is a prejudice in favor of or against one thing, person, or group when compared with another, usually in a way that is considered unfair. When you are biased, you are enacting this prejudice. Everyone has biases, whether we admit them or not. This chapter will teach you how to recognize your own biases, while chapter 7 will address how to recognize bias in what you read, listen to, and view.

Jim Taylor, a professor of psychology, describes biases as "distortions." He notes that historically they have served a purpose: "Biases must have had, at some point in our evolution, adaptive value. These distortions helped us to process information more quickly (e.g., stalking prey in the jungle), meet our most basic needs (e.g., help us find mates), and connect with others (e.g., be a part of a 'tribe')." He explains that in our more complex world, however, "the biases that helped us survive in primitive times when life was much simpler (e.g., life goal: live through the day) and speed of a decision rightfully trumped its absolute accuracy" are not as helpful. Instead, "correctness of information, thoroughness of processing, precision of interpretation, and soundness of judgment are, in most situations today, far more important than the simplest and fastest route to a judgment." In other words, because our world has changed so much, biases are no longer necessary or even helpful in our daily lives the way they were in primitive times. In fact, biases can prevent you from thinking in open and deliberate ways, which your instructor will likely expect you to do in your writing.

Biases become especially problematic when we are unaware of them, which can lead us to seek out information that continues to confirm our biases. This is called *confirmation bias*. Raymond S. Nickerson, a professor of psychology, explains confirmation bias: "Once one has taken a position on an issue, one's primary purpose becomes that of defending or justifying that position" (176). Thus "people tend to seek information that they consider supportive of favored hypotheses or existing beliefs and to interpret information in ways that are partial to those hypotheses or beliefs" (177). In other words, the very act of taking a position on an issue makes you single-mindedly committed to defending that position and to finding whatever evidence you can to support it. While it will be important for you to take a position in some of your writing assignments, you do not want to close yourself off to other positions or to evidence that conflicts with your position. In fact, acknowledging and responding to other positions and to evidence will help you develop more nuanced and complex positions.

Even when people do not seek information that supports their existing beliefs, the phenomenon of confirmation bias explains how they are able to find confirmation in evidence that opposes their beliefs. Foundational research on the subject demonstrates how people, even when confronted by evidence that disproves their position, "continue to reflect upon any information that suggests less damaging 'alternative inter-pretations.' Indeed, they may even come to regard the ambiguities and conceptual flaws in the data *opposing* their hypotheses as somehow sug-gestive of the fundamental *correctness* of those hypotheses" (Lord et al. 2099). In other words, "in everyday life . . . the mere availability of con-tradictory evidence rarely seems sufficient to cause us to abandon our prior beliefs or theories" (Lord et al. 2108). As you consider the evidence you are finding, remain aware of the phenomenon of confirmation bias. Also remember that algorithmic personalization and bias, discussed in chapter 2, will make it more difficult for you to locate content through search engines like *Google* that is different from content you searched for at an earlier date.

Cognitive Dissonance

Cognitive dissonance explains how people can believe conflicting posi-tions and act in simultaneously conflicting ways. Lawrence T. White, a professor of psychology, explains cognitive dissonance as follows:

> Psychological scientists have known for decades that we humans— and perhaps some primates—are motivated to maintain cognitive consistency. When we act in ways that are inconsistent with our atti-tudes and beliefs, we experience an aversive state of mental tension called cognitive dissonance. . . . Consider the teenager who starts smoking, even though she knows smoking causes cancer. Cognitive dissonance is a psychological consequence of that decision. Disso-nance is uncomfortable; it makes us feel like a hypocrite. So we take steps to eliminate the dissonance. We can change our behavior (*OK, I stopped smoking*) or we can change our belief (*hey, the claims about cigarettes causing cancer are overblown*).

In the example above, a teenager starts smoking even though she knows smoking causes cancer. That teenager will find ways to justify or ratio-nalize her choice so that she feels OK about smoking, even though it causes cancer. She may tell herself that she won't smoke for her whole life or will only smoke one cigarette a day. The point is that she will find ways to make herself feel good about her choice so that she doesn't feel the dissonance between her choice and what she knows are the consequences of that choice.

Let's consider another example of cognitive dissonance. Suppose one of your classmates (we'll call her Jane) does not believe that we should be concerned about the environment. It is a presidential election year, and she does not support the leading presidential candidate's proposed programs that give tax credits to drivers who trade in gas-guzzling trucks and SUVs for a more efficient vehicle or to homeowners who install solar panels to make their homes more energy efficient. Even though Jane does not vote for the candidate, the candidate wins. Within a year of the candidate's election, Jane has taken advantage of both programs. She walks away with a hefty tax credit for trading in her SUV and installing solar panels.

The theory of cognitive dissonance explains how Jane, on the one hand, votes against a candidate for developing energy-efficient programs but, on the other hand, takes advantage of those programs for personal gain. According to the theory, Jane will find a way to justify her actions. As you develop your source-driven projects, remain aware of inconsistencies in your thinking and attempts to justify and compensate for them.

Motivated Reasoning

Motivated reasoning explains the impulse to scrutinize ideas more carefully when we don't like them than when we do like them. This means that if we already believe something and are prompted to question it, we will not do so. On the other hand, if we don't believe something, we are more likely to look for flaws in its logic. Motivated reasoning also means that more and greater persuasion is needed to get people to change their minds (Petersen 1097). In other words, people are naturally inclined to believe what they want to believe, and so it is difficult to get people to change their minds. As the social psychologist Peter Ditto details, "Motivated reasoning is a pervasive tendency of human cognition. . . . People are capable of being thoughtful and rational, but our wishes, hopes, fears and motivations often tip the scales to make us more likely to accept something as true if it supports what we want to believe" (qtd. in Weir). As a researcher, writer, and thinker, you will want to be aware of this tendency to more readily accept ideas because they are consistent with your own. You will want to treat ideas that are consistent with your own ideas the same way that you would treat ideas inconsistent with your own, and you need to address both to develop complex and sophisticated projects.

Information Avoidance

Like the concepts mentioned above, information avoidance, another psychological phenomenon, is worth keeping in mind as you conduct your searches. *Information avoidance* is defined as "any behavior intended to prevent or delay the acquisition of available but potentially unwanted information" (Sweeny et al. 341). It can take many forms—for example, "asking someone not to reveal information, physically leaving a situation to avoid learning information, or simply failing to take the necessary steps to reveal the content of information" (Sweeny et al. 341). You can probably think of a time when you practiced information avoidance. Maybe you didn't want to think about a class you were afraid you were failing and so didn't check your grades online. Or maybe you refused to make an appointment for a medical test recommended by your doctor since it might have revealed that you were sick. The potential consequences of avoiding information depend, of course, on what kind of information you are avoiding. If you are avoiding viewpoints on a subject that challenge your own viewpoints, then one of the consequences could be that you appear closed-minded and miss the opportunity to think more complexly and fairly about a subject. This could be a problem when it comes to your writing and research assignments, for which you will likely be expected to engage and address opposing viewpoints. Avoiding information that conflicts with your own ideas will also likely pose problems for you outside school. If you are unwilling to entertain other peoples' viewpoints, whether in social situations, in the community, or in the workplace, you lose opportunities to engage in conversations that could expose you to and help you understand different perspectives on a given subject.

Recognizing Psychological Phenomena As You Read

Bias, cognitive dissonance, motivated reasoning, and information avoidance are some of the well-documented devices our brains use to protect our belief systems. Such devices may have evolved as survival strategies: motivated reasoning, for example, likely developed to "shield against manipulation" (Petersen 1097). Today, however, such protections constrain our ability to consider other perspectives and thus to develop new ideas. Although it's not always easy to do so, being aware of how these psychological phenomena limit you may help you counteract them and evolve as a thinker.

You can develop awareness by answering the following questions about what you read, hear, or see online:

- What was your first reaction to the material?
- Do you feel like challenging or confirming it?
- Do you feel compelled to share it with others?

Learn to recognize when you have strong emotional responses, whether positive or negative, because they cue these psychological phenomena to kick in.

✪ TRY IT

1. Understand what it means to read laterally.

Write a short summary describing the concept of reading laterally. What does one do while reading laterally? How is reading laterally different from reading vertically? What are thought to be the advantages of reading laterally?

2. Practice reading laterally.

Choose a website and evaluate its credibility by reading laterally. First, take your bearings and develop a plan. Then execute that plan. Where does your journey take you? What did you find out? Do you feel confident enough to offer an evaluation of the website? What evidence have you gathered to support your evaluation?

3. Practice recognizing your emotional responses to sources.

Go to the website of a group, organization, or political party with which you disagree. As you read the materials on the site, keep track of how you are responding emotionally to what you are reading. Does what you are feeling seem to exemplify one (or more) of the phenomena described in this chapter? Explain.

4. Address the implications of psychological phenomena on your research.

If you are involved in a research project, choose one of the psychological phenomena described in this chapter and anticipate the effect it could have on that project.

7

Exploring
the Credibility of Sources

RELATED APPENDIX ACTIVITIES: 2.2, 3.1, 3.2, 3.3

This chapter looks in more depth at how the credibility—that is, the trustworthiness—of a source can be determined by reading laterally, or across the web from site to site. It's important to understand that credibility is not stable. The credibility of an author, for example, can change over time. If someone was an expert on real estate ten years ago but has not kept up with relevant trends in the field, the person is no longer a credible source of information on real estate. Or perhaps a news publication used to win awards but has become lax in its adherence to sound journalistic practices. As a result, this publication's credibility has likely plummeted. This chapter addresses credibility as a complex concept but one that should enter into your assessment of sources.

Exploring an Author's Credibility

One of the elements that can support your assessment of a source is whether the author is trustworthy. *Author* here is a catchall term for the person or organization that created the source you're evaluating, whether the source is textual (like a news article), visual (like a video), or audio (like a podcast). While it's comforting to think that an author is either credible or not credible, this way of thinking oversimplifies things. For example, let's say you are researching heart disease. You find a blog post published on the personal website of a doctor who is a general practitioner— the kind of doctor you would visit if you had the flu—about treating patients with heart disease. That doctor may be credible in some contexts, since she went to medical school and likely has some experience working with patients with heart disease. But as the author of an informally published post on heart disease, a post that did not undergo review, she is not credible as an expert on the subject. More credible would be a peer-reviewed article in an academic journal written by a cardiologist—that is, a doctor with expertise in the treatment of heart diseases.

In other cases, authors may not be credible because they aren't up-to-date with research in their field, no matter how significantly they previously contributed to that field. For example, a researcher who made a groundbreaking discovery about genetic diseases in 1998 may not have been in a laboratory in fifteen years, which could affect her credibility when it comes to current information about genetic diseases. The point is that expertise itself is contextual. A person may be an expert in a specific field but not others or may have been an expert at one time but has since lost expertise as the field has changed. Reading laterally about the author by moving from site to site on the web will help you determine the extent to which the author's background, schooling, experience, and other credentials are trustworthy for your purposes.

You can also use *Google Scholar* to help you determine the credibility of an academic author. If you search *Google Scholar* for an author and article, you can find information on how often that article has been cited by others. A high number of citations is usually (although not always) a good indicator that authors are credible. A high number of citations may not be a good indicator of credibility, however, if the author is controversial and many of the citations actually debunk the author's theories. Also, you don't want to automatically assume that authors lack credibility if their articles have not been cited by many others. There are many reasons why this may happen: the author's articles may be new, may be on a very specific subject, may not have been indexed yet by *Google*, or may have been indexed incorrectly. In other words, don't just trust the numbers you find. The number of citations can give you some insight but should be considered alongside other information you collect about the author.

The website on which you find an author's work will also often provide information about the author. Sometimes you can click on the author's name to learn more. Other times, there will be an About section that will provide this information. Keep in mind that this section may be a useful starting point but that you will still want to read laterally to develop a comprehensive view of the author. The author's own website, the publisher's website, or the information about the author provided by the platform making the work available (usually supplied by the author or publisher) is likely to be biased in favor of the author's credibility.

Finally, like all of us, authors have biases. They have their own political beliefs, worldviews, values, professional and personal commitments, and life experiences that will necessarily influence what they write. It's important to recognize these biases as you are assessing an author's credibility so that you are aware of how biases inform the author's ideas.

Exploring a Source's Credibility through Publication Context

Context plays an important role in whether you should believe a source (though, certainly, there are objective facts that can be scientifically proved and that hold true across circumstances). The sources you locate will often be contained in a larger publication like a newspaper, academic journal, or website. The larger publication may have biases that will impact the credibility of its sources. The sources may be published by an organization that advocates for a particular cause or constituency, that espouses a political ideology, or that is funded or even owned by people intent on advancing an agenda instead of allowing contributors to have independence from that agenda.

Bias is especially important to consider with news sources, which ideally aim to be objective. In chapter 6, you read about how your biases can affect how you understand the world around you and your willingness to see things from other perspectives. Sources have biases too, and being aware of them will help you assess the credibility of what you find online.

Remember to read laterally to evaluate sources: What do other sites tend to say about the publication or site that published the source? Is the source considered to lean toward one ideological viewpoint? Are the publishers or owners of the publication said to influence its content and perspective? From there you can begin to piece together the biases of the larger context within which your source appears. Once you do so, you'll then want to ask yourself how these biases affect whether the source you have chosen is credible within the context of your project.

Let's consider an example. A website that is selling wooden cutting boards posts an article from *Cook's Magazine* about how wooden cutting boards are better than plastic cutting boards. The article's argument for using wooden cutting boards is that wood is a material known for its natural resistance to bacteria and, therefore, is not as susceptible as plastic to containing foodborne bacteria like salmonella. In other words, wooden cutting boards are safer than plastic ones. This piece from *Cook's Magazine* may very well be credible, but its presence on a site that is trying to sell you wooden cutting boards, a site that is clearly biased toward wood, should make you stop and think about how this bias might affect the article's credibility. In other words, you want to check out not only the credibility of the article and the magazine that originally published it by reading laterally but also the site that republished the article (in this case, a commercial site selling the product written about). Doing so will help you assess the article's credibility.

Let's look at an example of how to recognize bias when you are trying to learn about your sources. Perhaps you are writing a paper about successful strategies for business growth and use several quotations by a man named John Sniffern, the CEO of a big company, and you need to make sure that Sniffern is a credible source. You go to Sniffern's personal page on the company's website. It describes all of Sniffern's accomplishments, awards, and contributions to the company. Plus, there is a link to the company newsletter, where Sniffern is featured in a long, detailed cover story about his role in the growth of the company. All of this sounds very promising, and Sniffern comes off as credible, but think about how these sources—Sniffern's personal page on the company's website and the article about him in the company newsletter—are biased. It is in his company's best interest to paint its CEO in a positive light, celebrate his accomplishments, and point out his achievements. Sniffern may be credible, but these sources cannot be trusted because they are biased toward Sniffern. The personal page and company newsletter may be a place to start, but you would want to move outward from them and read laterally about Sniffern, from sources beyond his own company's, to gain multiple and more objective perspectives on him and the ideas he espouses. Maybe you find that he's won numerous awards, has been published in prestigious business journals, and has run other companies successfully using the same time-tested strategies.

Let's consider one final example. Perhaps you are interested in going skydiving and want to bring your brother along. Your brother is not as adventurous as you are and is scared to skydive. You send your brother to the website of the skydiving company, which addresses this common concern by assuring its readers (and potential customers) that fatalities and injuries while skydiving are uncommon. Is this company's website credible? Should your brother trust this information? The company may be offering accurate information, but remember that it is biased in favor of skydiving since that's what the company is selling. In other words, it is not in the company's interest to perpetuate your brother's fears, or your brother won't want to go skydiving. Alternatively, let's say that there is no information on the company's website about skydiving safety concerns. This shows bias, too. This kind of bias is called *bias by omission*. By leaving that information out, the company is showing its bias by not wanting to perpetuate fears about skydiving that may prevent you from purchasing the company's services. Either way, it is problematic to rely on this company's website for information about how safe skydiving is. Where can your brother go instead of the company's website to find the most accurate information?

Chapter 5 encourages you to find the primary source, but a primary source is not always available. In this case, your brother might look into whether there is an unbiased reference source, a secondary source, containing information about skydiving fatalities and injuries. Perhaps there is an organization that offers more credible information because it does not have a direct stake in whether someone skydives. Moving away from the company's website, you can look for a website along these lines. The website of a nonprofit organization like the United States Parachute Association (USPA) is likely a more credible source of this information, although it would be naive to think that such an organization has no financial stake in skydiving. Additional and potentially more objective information may be found through the United States Department of Transportation's Federal Aviation Administration (FAA), which regulates airspace usage. The FAA explains that

> sport parachuting has certain inherent risks for all participants. The FAA encourages sport parachutists to complete formal training courses offered by nationally recognized organizations or

organizations that have equivalent training programs. The United States Parachute Association (USPA) is an FAA-accepted, nationally recognized skydiving organization that licenses skydivers in the United States. . . . The USPA developed basic safety requirements and information for skydiving activities. These requirements and information are for training, checking equipment, and conducting a wide variety of sport parachuting activities. (2–3)

Whether you choose to rely on the information about skydiving safety you find on the USPA's site or the FAA's site, both are likely to be less biased than the information you find on a site that is selling skydiving trips. Moving away from the company's website and reading laterally to find other websites that may be less biased will be important in assessing the credibility of a source.

Recognizing Bias: A Closer Look

In the example about skydiving above, bias emerges in two ways. First, we can recognize that the company's website is biased toward skydiving because it is selling skydiving trips. Because of that commercial interest, the site is probably not the best source for objective information about how safe skydiving is. Second, if the site does not contain any information at all about the safety of skydiving, we can say that the source is biased by omission because it leaves out this information altogether.

Recognizing bias is important because you cannot make informed decisions if the information you rely on isn't credible. Remember that we are all biased in some way, and so too, to greater or lesser degrees, are our expressions.

Forms Bias Takes

Below is a list of the forms bias can take in a source. Keep these in mind as you read, listen to, and watch material online and in other digital environments.

OMISSION

Bias by omission, as discussed above, occurs when a source leaves out information that is relevant to the subject. The omitted information may conflict with the source's argument or may comprise quotations from experts or sources that have a different (and perhaps opposite) perspective on the subject. Even pertinent facts or statistics might be omitted. Simply put, bias by omission involves leaving out any information that does not support the position or goal of the source. In the case of bias by omission, what that source *doesn't* say is the key to recognizing its bias.

SELECTION

Whether you are engaging with a news story or reading sources for a research project, your sources will often quote other sources. You can recognize the bias of your source by paying attention to the other sources it quotes. Like in bias by omission, some sources will quote only sources that support their points instead of quoting sources with different perspectives on the subject. This shows bias. Similarly, if the source quotes experts, it is important to pay attention to what those experts say. Do they all share the same ideas, positions, and beliefs? If so, this may reveal the source's bias because the source does not include competing ideas, positions, and beliefs. This may suggest that the source's argument cannot stand up to opposing viewpoints or scrutiny of its methods and evidence. You also want to pay attention to the experts' affiliations, meaning that you should notice where they work, what their position is, and what groups (including political parties) they are affiliated with. Determining if the source includes more experts and sources that support one perspective over another can help you evaluate a source's bias.

EMPHASIS

Bias by emphasis can take various forms, but the underlying idea is that a source shows its bias by highlighting a specific perspective while downplaying other perspectives. For example, a news website might give visibility to stories that favor one political perspective by giving those stories better placement and bigger headlines and by publishing more of them.

What to Look For

Paying close attention to the language of what you are reading, viewing, or listening to can also reveal bias. Keep an eye out especially for over-statements and generalizations, loaded words, and labeling.

OVERSTATEMENTS AND GENERALIZATIONS

The words a source uses can reveal its biases. For example words like *always*, *never*, *all*, and *none* can lead to statements that are not true because they generalize or go too far. Such statements can indicate a bias because they do not leave space for other perspectives on the subject. You have likely heard many generalizations. Maybe you have heard that all girls like dolls or all rich people are greedy. Notice that all it takes is one girl who doesn't like a doll and one rich person who isn't greedy to show that these generalizations are untrue. If the word *all* was not included in these sentences, the generalization would be implied. Implicit or explicit, the generalization works the same way in both instances. Still, scanning for words that can lead to overstatements like those listed above can quickly draw your attention to moments when an author may be overstating the case. When it comes to bias, statements that go too far can alert you that the source you are reading is biased toward a specific point of view.

LOADED WORDS

As you notice word choice, also pay attention to the use of what are called *loaded words*, *charged words*, or *emotionally charged words*. These types of words are intended to evoke a feeling or emotion. Their use is an example of pathos (described in chapter 5) and can indicate a source's bias. The goal of loaded words is to create a reaction in you, whether positive or negative. For example, if you call someone *accomplished* or an *overachiever*, you are basically saying the same thing, but the term *overachiever* is loaded. It carries a negative connotation by suggesting that the achieving is excessive and thus indicates potential bias against the person it describes.

LABELING

Paying attention to how other sources and experts are described, or labeled, in your sources provides insight into bias. Like loaded words, labels often evoke a reaction. The kinds of labels used vary widely. You may notice labels like *conservative, liberal, feminist,* or *politician.* Keep in mind that many such labels are not biased in and of themselves. Instead, it's how a source uses them, as well as who gets labeled and who doesn't, that is important to observe. For example, imagine that a controversial speaker came to your school and some of the students challenged his presence, and the local newspaper wrote about it. Paying attention to how those students are labeled could help you detect bias. Are they called *protestors* or *troublemakers*? The term *protesters* has a more neutral connotation, perhaps even a positive one, while the term *troublemakers* has a negative connotation. Notice also the labels attached to the speaker. Is he described using political labels such as *conservative* or *liberal* or maybe even a more loaded label like *extremist*? Are political labels used to describe one side and not the other? Noticing the role of labels can help reveal the bias in what you read, listen to, and watch.

Understanding Media Bias

Part of judging the credibility of information and news you find online involves understanding its source. This has become increasingly difficult because there are so many media outlets that produce news and other information. While media outlets rarely identify themselves as liberal- or conservative-leaning, how they have reported various news stories over the years suggests their political biases. Figure 7.1 lays out one way of thinking about the most popular media outlets in terms of bias, locating the liberal-leaning outlets to the left and the conservative-leaning outlets to the right. The horizontal axis shows the potential bias of each outlet, while the vertical axis notes whether the outlet has a reputation for producing quality, credible news. This chart is seen as controversial by some people because of its classifications, and you, too, may disagree with the way some of the media outlets have been classified. Still, this chart may be a useful tool as you consider the potential biases in your sources. Whether you are relying on sources for a research paper or simply to back up your own opinion on a subject, you can pay attention to where your sources are located on this chart. If all your sources fall in one area on the chart you will likely want to consider incorporating

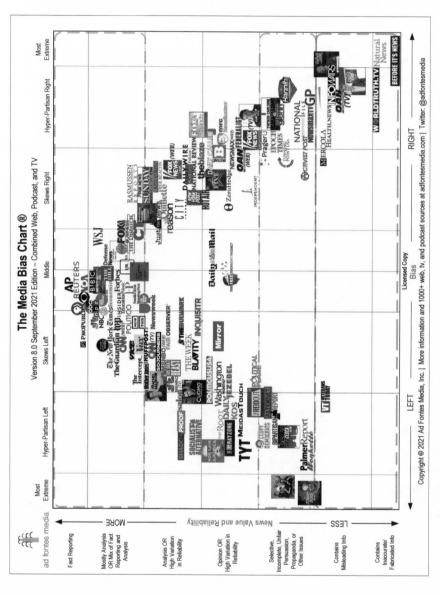

Fig. 7.1. Media bias chart, by Ad Fontes Media

sources located in other areas of the chart to offer a more balanced approach to your subject. You can read about the methodology behind this chart as well as the ongoing research supporting it at www.adfontesmedia.com/intro-to-the-media-bias-chart/.

What about the Credibility of *Wikipedia* and Other Wikis?

When you search the web, *Wikipedia* will often show up in your results toward the top of the list. *Wikipedia*—like all wikis—is a collaboratively written site that allows for the direct posting of content. Wikis may be private (which only certain people can contribute to) or public (which anyone can contribute to). The process for vetting information on wikis varies, typically occurs after publication, and in some cases is nonexistent. While you may have been told by your teachers never to use *Wikipedia*, there is really no reason to stay away from the site. The key to using *Wikipedia* productively is understanding how it works and when to use it. Because wikis, including *Wikipedia*, can be edited by anyone at any moment and thus the content may not have been verified by the community when you see it, you need to be careful about believing the material you find on wikis. As the eighth edition of the *MLA Handbook* notes, "Be sure to read the pages accompanying a *Wikipedia* entry, which give its history and the editors' discussions about it, since that information shows how the entry evolved and where the controversy in your subject lies" (12). As long as you approach *Wikipedia* with this in mind, it can be a valuable place to *begin* research—or to do what Randall McClure calls "presearch"—to get a broad sense of the subject and some useful and credible sources. But you should never end your research with *Wikipedia* or another wiki. Instead, use such sites at the very beginning stages of your research to gather basic information and sources and then move on to more credible sources.

Recognizing Misinformation and Disinformation

One of the principles that informs this guide is that being digitally literate will help you recognize misinformation and disinformation so that you can determine when information is credible. While the terms *misinformation* and *disinformation* are sometimes used interchangeably, they do not mean the same thing. While both terms describe information that is factually incorrect, the difference between the two is intent. As described in chapter 1, disinformation involves maliciously spreading wrong information, while misinformation is not spread with malicious intent. For example, you may have been misinformed about the deadline for registering for a promotion at your local movie theater, but it is doubtful that the representative at the theater spread incorrect information on purpose. That representative may have been misinformed and passed on that incorrect information to you.

A term you have probably heard that is meant to characterize disinformation is *fake news*. In fact, in 2017 a *Google* search for "fake news" yielded about five million hits. That's because in the months leading up to the 2016 presidential election in the United States, the term *fake news* began circulating widely after being used in *BuzzFeed* articles by the journalists Craig Silverman and Lawrence Alexander (Silverman; Silverman and Alexander). They noticed that fabricated news stories about the presidential election were appearing on a handful of websites, which could all be traced to Veles, Macedonia. The teenagers who created these websites saw the sites' popularity grow quickly and realized that they could make a lot of money from advertisers if the stories were shared widely on social media platforms. All in all, Silverman and Alexander found nearly two hundred of these sites trafficking in purely made-up news, most of which (although not all) revolved around the upcoming presidential election. The term *fake news*, however, is controversial: in fact, some people believe that it has been used to pit one political group against another and prefer the term *false news*.

Although the term *fake news* has currency—and may even have "gained an extra layer of meaning" in recent years according to one dictionary editor (Steinmetz)—it is worth remembering that fake news isn't a new or specifically American phenomenon. Satire, parody, propaganda, and false and misleading "news" stories have been around for hundreds of years. Fake news may sound like a simple concept, but it's in fact difficult to recognize and describe. As Wardle explains, "[T]he term fake doesn't begin to describe the complexity of the different types of misinformation (the inadvertent sharing of false information) and disinformation (the deliberate creation and sharing of information known to be false)" ("Fake News").

According to Wardle, there are three things worth paying attention to when it comes to news and information more generally: "the different types of content" (false, manipulated, and so on) and how the content was developed, the reason for its creation, and the method of sharing ("Fake News"). Figure 7.2 shows how these elements work together. As you can see, content might be made up, used to give an incorrect impression, delivered by a source that is not what it claims to be, or intended as satire or parody (as in *The Onion*, which may nonetheless mislead someone who fails to get the joke).

Figure 7.2 identifies other important aspects worth noticing when engaging with content—namely, whether it has been manipulated or put in an incorrect relation to other information. For example, the context may be false or the connections among the headlines, captions, and content may be inaccurate. Consider an article you might find on an entertainment news website. The headline promises a story about "Celebrities That Died without Anyone Knowing" and is accompanied by a photograph

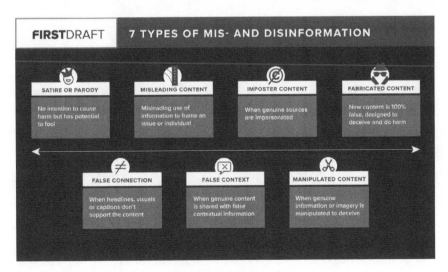

Fig. 7.2. Types of misinformation and disinformation

of a current celebrity who is (as far as you know) still living. The combination of the headline and picture suggests that the celebrity has died. Clicking on the article, however, you find out that the piece doesn't even mention that celebrity and, further, that the deaths mentioned in the article have, in fact, been reported widely. This is an example where the headline and photograph don't accurately represent the story attached to them. As discussed in chapter 10, articles like these can also be categorized as *clickbait* because they rely on sensational headlines that are not supported by the story you'll find once you click on the headline. Getting people to click on an article is not the only reason information might be put in an incorrect relation to other information: when intentionally done, the goal is to mislead, for any reason.

It is perhaps more difficult to determine whether something has been taken out of context and therefore may not be trustworthy. While a photograph or video may be real, the context within which it is being presented may not be accurate. When photographs or videos are particularly dramatic, they often go viral and lack context. For example, a video of the 2018 Thai cave rescue operation of a team of youth soccer players that went viral turned out to be footage from a cave dive in 2012 filmed in Wisconsin. The video had not been manipulated, but the context had. Chapter 9 will give you some tools and strategies for conducting reverse searches to determine the origins of online images and videos.

Digital media and related technologies allow disinformation to be created with ease and to spread widely and quickly. Yet recent studies show that human beings are still the primary reason for the spread of disinformation. One such study looked at the circulation of true and false news online and found that "contrary to conventional wisdom, robots accelerated the spread of true and false news at the same rate, implying that false news spreads more than the truth because humans, not robots, are more likely to spread it." The researchers conclude that "human behavior contributes more to the differential spread of falsity and truth than automated robots do" and advise that "understanding how false news spreads is the first step toward containing it" (Vosoughi et al. 1146). In other words, understanding how disinformation spreads can help you limit its spread.

Unfortunately, a more recent study indicates that three in four Americans overestimate their ability to distinguish false news from legitimate news and, moreover, that these overconfident individuals report greater willingness to share and spread this content on social media. People in this population are also the least aware of their own limitations (Lyons et al.). These findings suggest the importance of being honest with yourself about your own abilities to recognize fake news and the need to hone these abilities. After all, statistically speaking, it's more likely than not that you fall within the seventy-five percent of overconfident Americans who believe they can spot fake news.

✿ TRY IT

1. Practice determining an author's credibility.

Locate the author of something you are reading for a class or for pleasure. Read laterally to determine the author's credibility as it relates to the text you are reading. What kind of sources did you find? What do the sources you found reveal about the author? Is the author credible when it comes to the subject they are writing about?

2. Practice determining sources' biases.

Imagine you are writing a history of your hometown. Begin conducting a search for publications that will help you do so. Keep track of the potential biases of the sources you find. For example, what biases might an advertisement for your hometown have?

3. Pay attention to an author's word choice.

Read the following word pairs and indicate which is the more loaded choice. Explain why.

cabin	shack
calmed	neutralized
exploit	benefit from
adventure	escapade
selective	picky
confident	arrogant
vintage	old

4. Notice labeling.

Read the following paragraph and make a list of all the labels used in it. Then, write a short piece about the biases that these labels may indicate.

> A recent survey conducted by a nonpartisan polling organization indicates that there remains a bias against hiring women to work in scientific fields. The study reported on the hiring practices of five different universities. Hiring committees composed of both male and female scientists read twenty applications for a position as a researcher in one of the campus laboratories. The applications were exactly the same except half had traditionally male names on them and the other half had traditionally female names on them. In all instances—at all five universities—the male applicants were ranked over the female applicants despite containing the same information. John Delgone, chair of the biology department at Harsen University, one of the institutions that participated in the study, explained, "This study clearly shows that we must review our own biases in the sciences and strive to diversify our field." Dan Browning, director of the Human Genome Institute at another one of the participating universities, similarly noted, "I deeply regret how this played out. I did not expect that the applications from females would be treated any differently, but the study shows otherwise. We must look inside ourselves and really think about what this says about our field." The feminist Dana Lyons, who teaches in the physics department at another participating school, responded to the study noting that it "underscores that bias and prejudice against women are still alive and well." Apologizing for his role in what he sees as "sexism at its worst," Lars Norgun, professor of physics, noted, "I will address the findings of this study with members of future hiring committees so this doesn't happen again."

5. Explore *Wikipedia*.

Go to an entry of your choice on *Wikipedia*. Read the entry and then review any available footnotes or bibliography entries. Choose one credible source (determining its credibility by reading laterally) and compare it to the *Wikipedia* entry. What does *Wikipedia* get right and what does it get wrong?

 READ ABOUT IT

In this chapter you read about misinformation and disinformation as well as the use of the term *fake news* to describe disinformation. With that section in mind, now read John Maxwell Hamilton and Heidi Tworek's "A Real History of Fake News" and answer the questions following the selection.

John Maxwell Hamilton is Hopkins P. Breazeale Professor of Journalism at Louisiana State University's Manship School of Mass Communication, and Heidi Tworek is associate professor, jointly appointed at the School of Public Policy and Global Affairs and in the Department of History at the University of British Columbia. In "A Real History of Fake News," Hamilton and Tworek consider early manifestations of fake news to show that fake news emerged simultaneously alongside the very first newspapers as early as 1622.

A Real History of Fake News
John Maxwell Hamilton and Heidi Tworek

> 1 Herald: News, news, news!
> 2 Herald: Bold and brave news.
> 1 Herald: New as the night they are born in.
> 2 Herald: Or the phant'sie that begot 'em.
> —Ben Jonson, *News of the New World*

If the past half-dozen years have a defining concept, it may be the refrain "fake news," a phrase that former President Donald Trump claims to have invented. In the last year alone, books with those pungent two words in the title have described beauty pageants, theology, pregnancy, clinical engineering, sports (Jones), and, of course, politics.

"From 2016 onwards, the political state of play has changed—disinformation narratives are how you play elections," said one researcher in November 2020 (Murphy and Venkataramakrishnan). In 2016 the State Department created the Global Engagement Center, whose mission is to "lead, synchronize, and coordinate efforts of the Federal Government to recognize, understand, expose, and counter foreign state and non-state propaganda and disinformation efforts aimed at undermining United States national security interests."

But is fake news really news? In one sense, perhaps. Technological advances that enable the dissemination of fake news have themselves accelerated. In the process, politicians have learned to throw the term "fake news" around indiscriminately, as when another President, Richard Nixon, repeatedly hauled out the phrase "national security" to dismiss the Watergate investigation and other inconvenient inquiries into his administration's activities.

In another sense, though, fake news is not novel at all. It was widespread from the very beginning of newspapers as we know them. In fact, the long and broad history of faking is an uncomfortably integral part of the news itself.

A convenient starting point is 1622, when a London printer named Nathaniel Butter made journalism history by starting the first British newspaper. This was a step forward from the so-called manuscript news services previously available to gentry and political leaders, who could hire someone to compile snippets of current affairs information from abroad. Now, thanks to Butter, many people could imbibe the news.

The seed of Butter's *Certain News of the Present Week* grew into a flourishing news industry that enlarged the sphere of public discourse in England. The process occurred in other countries as well. The thought took hold that knowledge-empowered citizens would produce better societies. "From little compartments of the type case [sic] in printing shops, great and generous ideas will come forth," said Louis-Sébastien Mercier, a keen observer of French politics in the 1780s, "and it will be impossible for man to resist them." With gushing enthusiasm over this development, he prophesied, "Everything had a general and clearly distinguishable tendency toward perfection." By the 19th century, members of the British Parliament expressed concern that they no longer held much power to lead, given the sway of journalism over British subjects' opinions.

These same ideas washed up on the shores of the United States. Thomas Jefferson, among other Founding Fathers, said the press was more valuable than government itself. "Were it left to me to decide whether we should have government without newspapers," he said, "or newspapers without a government, I should not hesitate a moment to prefer the latter." The 1792 Postal Service Act subsidized the exchange of newspapers through the mail, enabling the cheap movement of information. "Of all the countries in the world," Alexis de Tocqueville noted in the early 1830s, "America is the one with both the most associations and the most newspapers."

But something else about Butter's newspaper endured as well. *The News of this Present Week* was disreputable. It was not just that Butter had a shaky grasp on grammar and proofreading. Nor was it his inconsistency in deciding what constituted news. (He could not even make up his mind as to what to call his newspaper, which also appeared as *The Last News*, *More News*, and *Brief Abstracts out of Divers Letters of Trust, Relating the News of the Present Week*.) Indeed, the problem was even more profound than any of those shortcomings. It was that when Butter published something that was not trivial, it was often made up.

This, too, would take hold with other newspapers. In one of his less optimistic pronouncements about the press, Jefferson said, "Nothing can now be believed which is seen in a newspaper. Truth itself becomes suspicious by being put into that polluted vehicle."

Perhaps the first critic of disreputable "faking" was Butter's contemporary, the playwright Ben Jonson. Not long before Butter printed his first weekly—on Fleet Street, which would become London's newspaper district—Jonson, in *News of the New World*, from which the quote at the top of this essay is taken, noted the "curious uncertainties" that pervaded manuscript news services. Five years later, Jonson attacked Butter directly in a satirical play called *The Staple of News*. Thus, an innovation that promised greater enlightenment arrived hand-in-hand with confusion, derision, and fear.

Despite Donald Trump's claim that he invented the term "fake news," it can be found in newspapers in the 19th century. Here is an item from the *Los Angeles Times* of May 15, 1891: "The City of Mexico promises to eclipse the reputation which Willcox, Ariz., held during the Geronimo outbreak as a manufacturing point for fake news." Around the same time, books appeared with titles like *Fakes in American Journalism* (1914) and *Facts and Fakes About Cuba* (1897). The former was written by a socialist who thought the press did not treat his political point of view with sufficient sympathy. The latter exposed the false news that American correspondents served up about the Spanish-American War.

The fakery was not confined to political reporting. Medical advertising was ubiquitous in the 19th and early 20th centuries, with many suppliers promising impossible results. Until the Food and Drug Administration (FDA) began regulating the field after its establishment in 1906, overblown claims about miracle cures provided a significant portion of newspapers' revenues.

This history is worth recalling when we look at the mounting contemporary concerns over fake news. True, technology has contributed to the proliferation of bogus information. Today, fake news travels far and wide in the blink of an eye. Technology also allows for anonymous reporting, which means that "journalists" who purvey the "news" do not have to take heat for their actions.

But, as powerful as technology is, the roots of fake news lie in human nature. On the eve of the Enlightenment, as masses of people acquired greater ability to think for themselves, uncover facts, and report them, they often found it more fun and profitable to make things up, as Butter did.

The rise of fact-based journalism in the 20th century helped curb these excesses. The costs of entry into newspaper publishing soared, something that Upton Sinclair decried in 1919 in his muckraking *The Brass Check*. (The brass check reference was to tokens given to women in brothels for their services.) Few could afford to buy expensive presses and populate newsrooms with talented reporters. The newspapers that thrived became more professional, not only because journalists liked the idea (they were respected and paid more) but also because owners found it good business to provide high-quality news. Although this news was not without many flaws and the coverage not without lacunae, its relative reliability attracted advertisers who sought credibility.

This economic model is now broken, thanks in part to technological change. Advertisers don't need newspapers in the way they did before. More, the hegemony of principled editors over the news has eroded. Once upon a time, no newspaper would publish a story claiming that Hillary Clinton was running a child sex ring out of a pizza parlor. Now, even the best newspapers are obliged to report about the story, at least to discredit it, lest they seem detached from public discourse.

This brings us to another human factor. People have long glommed onto news that confirms what they think is true. Germans believed that Kaiser Wilhelm II had abdicated on November 9, 1918, because it made sense in the dying days of World War I. In fact, the news was spread by Chancellor Max von Baden, who wanted to forestall revolution in Berlin. The Kaiser did not actually abdicate until weeks later, from his base in exile in the Netherlands. But because the abdication story made intuitive sense, many history books still repeat the false narrative about the Kaiser's abdication.

When *The New York Times* tries to discredit fake news, it often achieves the opposite result: Readers are reminded of the original story, and those who believed it before are likely to be reinforced in their view. After all, if you believe that Hillary Clinton is into sex trafficking, you are likely to think *The New York Times* is happy to cover it up.

History tells us that faking is here to stay. An excellent reading list for students by Alice Marwick, Rachel Kuo, Shanice Cameron, and Moira Weigel highlights the fact that disinformation shaped the United States from its foundation and has been continually intertwined with race, even up to anti-Asian sentiment during Covid-19. Meanwhile, although the FDA has largely rid newspapers of medical disinformation, such disinformation continues to exist and wreak havoc. Purdue Pharma spent six to twelve times as much money promoting OxyContin to physicians than Purdue's competitors did for their products, contributing to OxyContin's prominent success (Van Zee n19). Erroneous claims about its non-addictive nature helped fuel a proliferation of prescriptions. Medical disinformation spread an opioid epidemic that has claimed over five hundred thousand American lives.

This history does not mean that improvement is hopeless, but improvement will not come unless root causes of fakery are considered.

Many commentators have pointed to foreign interference and geopolitics as factors in misinformation. While these are part of the story, the history suggests two other crucial factors. The first is economics: People fake because it makes money for them. Some people, like Alex

Jones, have combined political disinformation with the sale of superfluous vitamin supplements (Warzel).

The second factor is the underlying domestic political situation: Researchers have shown that Americans disseminate more fake news because of polarized partisanship than they do for other reasons (Osmundsen et al.). This partisan motivation may be exacerbated by the design of social media, but social media did not cause polarization (Bail). As Daniel Kreiss and Shannon McGregor have pointed out, we need to address racial inequalities and other problems in U.S. society rather than just "reactively blaming technology for democratic problems."

Social media platforms can and should address the economic motivations behind faking. But it is up to politicians and citizens to improve the civic health of American society.

Works Cited

Bail, Chris. *Breaking the Social Media Prism*. Princeton UP, 2021.

Jones, Patrick. *Did the Truth Even Matter? Fake News, Felons and Football: Book Two*. Andrew Thorton Publishing, 2021.

Kreiss, Daniel, and Shannon McGregor. "Polarization Isn't America's Biggest Problem—Or Facebook's." *Wired*, 5 Apr. 2021, www.wired.com/story/polarization-isnt-americas-biggest-problem-or-facebooks/.

Marwick, Alice, et al. *Critical Disinformation Studies: A Syllabus*. Center for Information, Technology, and Public Life (CITAP), U of North Carolina, Chapel Hill, 2021, citap.unc.edu/critical-disinfo.

Murphy, Hannah, and Siddharth Venkataramakrishnan. "Conspiracy and Disinformation: America's New Politics." *Financial Times*, 13 Nov. 2020, www.ft.com/content/c30796ca-060d-42c0-b8e0-64e401e5193d.

Osmundsen, Mathias, et al. "How Partisan Polarization Drives the Spread of Fake News." *Brookings*, 13 May 2021, www.brookings.edu/techstream/how-partisan-polarization-drives-the-spread-of-fake-news/.

Van Zee, Art. "The Promotion and Marketing of Oxycontin: Commercial Triumph, Public Health Tragedy." *American Journal of Public Health*, vol. 99, no. 2, 2009, pp. 221–27. *PubMed Central*, www.ncbi.nlm.nih.gov/pmc/articles/PMC2622774.

Warzel, Charlie. "We Sent Alex Jones' Infowars Supplements to a Lab. Here's What's In Them." *BuzzFeed*, 9 Aug. 2017, www.buzzfeednews.com/article/ charliewarzel/we-sent-alex-jones-infowars-supplements-to-a-lab-heres.

"A Real History of Fake News" Reading Questions

1. This reading discusses fake news from a historical perspective. What does this historical perspective help us understand about our contemporary moment and the role of disinformation in it? Why does this matter?

2. In this article, the fatal results of medical disinformation are discussed. List a few additional contemporary examples of the consequences of the spread of disinformation.

3. John Maxwell Hamilton and Heidi Tworek note that "the roots of fake news lie in human nature." What do they mean by this, and what role does human nature play in the other roots they describe?

8

Working
with Your Sources

RELATED APPENDIX ACTIVITIES: 3.2, 3.3

So far, this book has mainly focused on how you locate and assess sources: the first steps in any research process, whether you're writing a paper for class or trying to answer an everyday question. At some point you will need to do something with your sources. For example, you might be asked to respond to your sources, challenge the ideas in your sources, use your sources to support your ideas, synthesize your sources, or compare and contrast your sources. While your instructor will likely provide you with various assignments and prompts, this chapter addresses some of the most common ways students are expected to engage with sources.

How to Use Sources

If someone asked you why you cite sources, you would likely say to support your points. Sources can certainly be used to bolster your points, but there is a range of other ways that sources can be used. This list reviews some of those ways so that you can think more complexly about how the sources you have located can be used in your projects. Consider using your sources to

- expand and enrich your own ideas about the subject
- complicate and challenge your own ideas about the subject
- identify differences between your ideas and the source's ideas
- define key terms related to the subject
- offer background information on the subject

- juxtapose ideas from multiple sources to produce new knowledge
- introduce a new perspective or way of framing the subject
- show that your writing doesn't depend only on opinion
- establish your credibility
- meet the expectations and conventions of your discipline

In figure 8.1 at the end of this chapter an excerpt from a sample essay on deforestation shows how sources may be used in some of these ways.

Synthesizing Your Sources

In addition to using sources individually in the ways listed above, your instructor may expect you to synthesize your sources. To *synthesize* means to bring together. Thus, synthesizing sources means bringing sources together. You usually bring together sources on the same subject to explore that subject more deeply. Your instructor may also ask that you find a place for your own ideas as you synthesize your sources. You may be asked to respond to the sources or to develop a thesis statement that will guide your synthesis.

To synthesize your sources, you will need to understand what each source says. You can refer to the strategies in chapter 5, which will support your comprehension of both text-based and visual sources. Once you are sure you understand the ideas belonging to each source, you will need to bring those sources together by thinking about how they relate to one another. Do the sources take the same or different positions on the subject? Do they address the subject from similar or differing perspectives? Does one source serve as an example of what the other source is arguing? As you synthesize your sources, your instructor will likely expect that you quote or paraphrase from each source so that you accurately represent what each says.

The next step in synthesizing is to think about your response to the sources and the reason for your reaction. Responding may begin with agreeing or disagreeing, but in an academic context you will need to do even more if you are going to participate in a sophisticated way. The following steps allow you to contribute your own ideas to the synthesis and use sources to do more than support your points (a similar list appears in chapter 3 of Carillo, *A Writer's Guide*):

1. Take a point further by considering its implications and additional evidence.

2. Redefine the context of the conversation.

3. Explore different implications for the findings.

4. Complicate an argument.

5. Locate a fault (an unfounded assumption, for example) and remedy it.

6. Explore why a particular approach is limiting and apply an alternative approach.

7. Redefine some of the terms or ideas offered.

8. Raise unexplored questions and their significance.

Avoiding Plagiarism

No matter how you end up using your sources, you must be sure not to plagiarize. Plagiarizing is the act of using ideas or language that is not your own, like the language and ideas from a source, without giving that source credit. Students plagiarize for a range of reasons, but sometimes plagiarism is unintentional, which means the student didn't mean to plagiarize. In some cases, students aren't aware that they must cite all their sources, including for images and graphics, or they may not know how to do so correctly.

As you locate and work with your sources, therefore, it is important to make sure you save all the information you will need to cite your sources correctly. Your instructor will likely ask you to use MLA format or some other documentation practice. This is another place where reference management software and research management platforms can be helpful. Because these tools allow you to stay organized and keep track of your sources (and the ideas in each source), you will be able to clearly distinguish your source's ideas from your own ideas.

✿ TRY IT

1. Explore how an author uses sources.

Choose one of the readings from this guide or something you are reading for another class that contains quotations from multiple sources. Referring to the list at the beginning of this chapter under "How to Use Sources," keep track of how the author uses sources. You may annotate the text by writing notes in the margin or on a separate sheet of paper, or by typing them up.

2. Explore how an author contributes ideas to a conversation.

Choose one of the readings from this guide or something you are reading for another class that contains quotations from multiple sources. Referring to the list in this chapter under "Synthesizing Your Sources," keep track of the moves the author makes to contribute ideas to the conversation about the subject. You may annotate the text by writing notes in the margin or on a separate sheet of paper, or by typing them up.

3. Practice using sources for more than support.

Choose three ways you can use sources from the list "Synthesizing Your Sources" in this chapter, and try these out in the next source-based piece of writing you compose.

4. Annotate to reflect on your use of sources.

Once you have completed Try It activity 3 above, annotate your writing (like the model in figure 8.1) to show where you are using sources in these ways.

5. Conduct research about how a discipline uses sources.

A discipline is a field of study like biology, English, or psychology. While you may not know which field you are going to major in or eventually work in, choose one that interests you, and use your library's catalog or database to locate an academic journal in that field. Choose an article in the journal. Although you may not understand all the content since the article is likely written for experts in the field, read through the piece paying attention to how sources are used. Referring to the list under "How to Use Sources" in this chapter, take notes on where and why the author incorporates each source into the piece. What preliminary answers can you give to the question, How are sources used by the author?

Fig. 8.1. Excerpt showing how sources may be used

In recent years, the increase in the human population has led to the need to construct more housing. Much of this construction is happening in our world's forests, which "cover 31% of the land area on our planet" ("Deforestation and Forest Degradation"). Cutting down forests to build homes or for other reasons is called deforestation. Deforestation is defined as "the permanent destruction of forests in order to make the land available for other uses" (Bradford) and has been described as a "consequence of population growth— more people, more food required, more land for cultivation and grazing" (Hartwick 155). The rate at which deforestation is happening is alarming. Christina Nunez explains that between 1990 and 2016 "the world lost 502,000 square miles (1.3 million square kilometers) of forest, according to the World Bank—an area larger than South Africa." While deforestation negatively impacts the plants and animals that depend on forests for their habitats, it is also largely considered one of the primary contributors to climate change. Although we cannot control the rise of the human population, we can be more aware of deforestation and its effects on different species, as well as on climate change.

> The source provides background information.

> The source defines a key term.

> The source supports the previous point.

The World Wildlife Fund explains that forests play an important role in "mitigating climate change because they act as a carbon sink—soaking up carbon dioxide that would otherwise be free in the atmosphere and contribute to ongoing changes in climate patterns" ("Deforestation and Forest Degradation"). This means that without forests the levels of carbon dioxide in the atmosphere are not controlled. In fact, as the Earth Day Network's website explains, "Combatting deforestation has been identified as one of the most promising and cost-effective ways to lower emissions" and can be done by "halting the loss and degradation of natural systems and promoting their restoration" ("Deforestation and Climate Change"). In other words, humans can make decisions and support policies that advance these ways of lowering emissions.

> The source provides background information.

> Sources in this and the following paragraph show that these ideas are not just based on opinion.

Deforestation has also meant the endangerment and extinction of many species. Nunez writes, "Eighty percent of Earth's land animals and plants live in forests, and deforestation threatens species including the orangutan, Sumatran tiger, and many species of birds." The Center for Biological Diversity details that while natural events such as "asteroid strikes, volcanic eruptions, and natural climate shifts" are to blame for previous extinctions (like the extinction of dinosaurs), the "current crisis is almost entirely caused by us—humans. In fact, ninety-nine percent of currently threatened species are at risk from human activities, primarily those driving habitat loss, introduction of exotic species, and global warming" ("The Extinction Crisis"). This comparison between the causes of endangerment

> The source provides information that enriches the overall understanding of the subject.

(continued on next page)

Fig. 8.1. (*cont'd*)

and extinction is important because it helps us understand the major role that humans are playing in this crisis today and suggests that we have the ability to control and to slow this crisis, if not stop it altogether.

Despite these severe consequences of deforestation, some people are skeptical about not just the effects of deforestation but climate change generally. Writing for *InfoWars*, Dan Lyman cites the former Environmental Protection Agency administrator Scott Pruitt's statement that "scientists continue to disagree about the degree and extent of global warming and its connection to the actions of mankind." Taking this point even further, Patrick Henningsen, also writing for *InfoWars*, notes, "The global warming and climate change mythology continues to spiral down into irrelevancy." While Pruitt suggests that climate change may or may not be occurring, Henningsen outright refers to climate change as a myth. Despite these opinions, as of 2016, more than ninety-seven percent of scientists who study climate change and most of the leading scientific organizations worldwide agree that the warming trends and related issues are the result of climate change, which is due largely to human activities ("Scientific Consensus"). It's hard to ignore that data when those skeptical of climate change don't seem to have any data to support their opinions.

> Two sources from *InfoWars* complicate and challenge the argument about climate change.

> Juxtaposing this source and the two from *InfoWars* reveals the lack of data in the *InfoWars* sources.

Works Cited

Bradford, Alina. "Deforestation: Facts, Causes & Effects." *Live Science*, 3 Apr. 2018, www .livescience.com/27692-deforestation.html.

"Deforestation and Climate Change." *Earth Day Network*, www.earthday.org/campaigns/ reforestation/deforestation-climate-change/. Accessed 29 May 2018.

"Deforestation and Forest Degradation." *World Wildlife Fund*, www.worldwildlife.org/threats/ deforestation-and-forest-degradation. Accessed 29 May 2018.

"The Extinction Crisis." *Center for Biological Diversity*, www.biologicaldiversity.org/programs/ biodiversity/elements_of_biodiversity/extinction_crisis/. Accessed 29 May 2018.

Hartwick, John M. "Deforestation and Population Increase." *Institutions, Sustainability, and Natural Resources: Institutions for Sustainable Forest Management*, edited by Sashi Kant and R. Albert Berry, Springer, 2005, pp. 155–92.

Henningsen, Patrick. "The Ultimate Green Bombshell: New Study Finds That Wind Farms Cause Actual Climate Change." *InfoWars*, 30 Apr. 2012, www.infowars.com/the -ultimate-green-bombshell-new-study-finds-wind-farms-cause-actual-climate-change/.

Lyman, Dan. "Climate Changists Throwing Fits over Trump's EPA Pick." *InfoWars*, 8 Dec. 2016, www.infowars.com/climate-changists-throwing-fits-over-trumps-epa-pick/.

Nunez, Christina. "Climate 101: Deforestation." *National Geographic*, 7 Feb. 2019, www .nationalgeographic.com/environment/global-warming/deforestation/.

"Scientific Consensus." *Global Climate Change: Vital Signs of the Planet*, NASA, climate.nasa .gov/scientific-consensus/. Accessed 29 May 2018.

9

Additional Strategies and Resources

This chapter provides strategies for developing your web-navigation skills and information about using fact-checking websites, doing reverse searches, dealing with defunct websites, and taking control of your online experience.

Fact-Checking Websites

Of the many fact-checking websites online, some cover general topics of interest in the news and on social media, and others focus primarily on political stories. The sites listed below are credible and can be helpful as you read laterally, but be aware that some have biases that may not be readily visible.

Snopes

One of the most popular fact-checking websites, *Snopes* (www.snopes .com) was initially founded in 1994 to debunk urban legends. In recent years, *Snopes* has become a well-respected fact-checking site that tells readers whether news stories and other claims circulating widely in the media are trustworthy. It also aggregates news stories. The site is independently run and nonpartisan, meaning that it is not affiliated with any political party and doesn't lean toward either liberal or conservative viewpoints. If you are reading laterally, go to *Snopes* to see if the source you have found appears on the site. A quick check on the site might save you a lot of time!

PolitiFact

PolitiFact (www.politifact.com) is a Pulitzer Prize–winning fact-checking website. Using the Truth-o-Meter, it rates the accuracy of statements made by people in politics in the United States as *true, mostly true, half true, mostly false,* or *false.* The site reserves one additional category for the biggest falsehoods, which it calls *pants on fire!* Run by reporters and editors from the independent newspaper the *Tampa Bay Times, PolitiFact* is generally considered unbiased.

FactCheck

FactCheck (www.factcheck.org) is published by the Annenberg Public Policy Center of the University of Pennsylvania. It is a nonpartisan, nonprofit fact-checking website that monitors the accuracy of statements made by those in politics in the United States. It is generally considered unbiased.

Fact Checker

Fact Checker is part of another publication: *The Washington Post* (www.washingtonpost.com/news/fact-checker/). The fact-checking websites that have appeared on this list so far are nonpartisan. However, while *Fact Checker*'s fact-checking work is detailed, well-sourced, and generally respected, it has been accused of checking claims made by conservatives more often than those made by liberals, and thus some consider it to have a liberal-leaning bias.

Media Matters for America

Media Matters for America (www.mediamatters.org) is a nonprofit research and information center that is openly liberal in its bias in that it focuses on fact-checking "conservative misinformation—news or commentary that is not accurate, reliable, or credible and that forwards the conservative agenda." It was launched in May 2004 ("About").

NewsBusters

NewsBusters (www.newsbusters.org) is a project of the conservative Media Research Center. It focuses on "exposing and combatting liberal media bias." Launched about a year after *Media Matters*, *NewsBusters* aims "to provide immediate exposure of national media bias, unfairness, inaccuracy, and occasional idiocy" and calls itself "America's leading media watchdog in documenting, exposing and neutralizing liberal media bias" ("About NewsBusters.org").

As you read laterally, these and other fact-checking sites can support your evaluation of sources. Keep in mind, though, that while some of these sites are independent and nonpartisan, others have an explicit bias. Using both kinds of sites in tandem can help you develop a more comprehensive and objective understanding of your sources. The About or other informational section of fact-checking sites may reveal their political leanings. If the site does not openly address its biases, then you can read laterally to help determine biases.

Conducting Reverse Searches

When you conduct a reverse search, you begin with the image, website, or social media account and work backward to figure out its source or who owns it. Doing reverse searches is important for the same reason that finding the primary source is important: a reverse search directs you to the original, which has not been filtered through another site or source. (In chapter 5, you read about primary and secondary sources: primary sources are original documents, whereas secondary sources are *about* original documents.) Locating the original source of a derivative or manipulated version of that source—or locating the owner of a website or social media account—can help you evaluate the credibility of what you have in front of you.

Not all images, websites, or social media accounts are up-front about their origin, purpose, authorship, and sponsorship, which is why the skill of reverse searching is worth honing. A social media account might indicate that it belongs to one person, but you might notice that the viewpoints expressed on it do not seem to fit with other viewpoints that person has expressed. For example, perhaps a congresswoman's *Twitter* account expresses views that are totally opposed to the platform she has been running on. This may suggest that a political competitor or detractor is trying to undermine the congresswoman's credibility and her commitment to her chosen causes. Similarly, a *Facebook* page claiming to belong to the American Academy of Pediatrics that includes articles about how children don't need pediatricians (doctors who specialize in children's medicine) and can get comparable treatment from nonspecialists would likely not belong to the American Academy of Pediatrics; the page advocates for something in direct conflict with the purpose of the association. Perhaps a group that is trying to cut down health-care costs has created a *Facebook* account that masquerades as one belonging to the American Academy of Pediatrics. You can do a reverse search to determine who really owns the account.

Reverse searches are also important if you are interested in including an image in one of your projects because you need to be sure you know where that image is from so you can assess its credibility. And, as you have likely surmised by now, knowing who is behind a website can help you judge its credibility as you move outward from that website and read laterally. Let's look at how to conduct these different kinds of reverse searches.

Conducting a Reverse Image Search

While there are specific websites and applications dedicated to helping you conduct reverse image searches, one of the easiest ways to do so is by using *Google*. *Google*'s support pages provide instructions detailing four ways of conducting a reverse image search. At the time of this writing, the simplest method on a computer running the *Chrome* browser is to right-click on the image. You can find instructions from *Google* for conducting reverse image searches on a computer, tablet, or phone (support .google.com/websearch/answer/1325808?hl=en).

When you conduct a reverse image search, your results will contain a list of the places on the web where the image (potentially in different sizes and formats) is located, as well as where similar images are located. Let's look at an example of a photograph that circulated in early June 2020 when occupation protesters in Seattle took over about six city blocks and declared the space to be the Capitol Hill Autonomous Zone (fig. 9.1). The photograph, published by Fox News on its website's home page, shows a man running in the street between burning buildings and a burning car. Some Internet browsers, such as *Chrome*, will allow you to right-click on the image and choose "Search image with Google Lens." The search returns a slew of stories about this manipulated image, including the original photograph, which was actually taken weeks before in Minneapolis, Minnesota. Not only was the photograph taken before the Capitol Hill Autonomous Zone was established, the photo was taken in a different city altogether. Fox News apologized for publishing this image and the series of other manipulated images it admitted to using in its coverage of the protests in Seattle. Reading laterally to locate the original source of this photograph reveals that the photograph was taken out of its original context. Had you viewed the photograph only in isolation and read vertically, you may have been duped. After all, it is a real photograph. Only when you read laterally do you discover that Fox News misrepresents both where and when the photograph was taken.

Fig. 9.1. Image published out of context by Fox News

Conducting a Reverse Website Search

A reverse website search helps you determine who owns a site. It is conducted using the website address (the URL, like reddit.com) or the IP address (that is, the Internet protocol address, a unique string of numbers separated by periods that identifies each device using the protocol to communicate over a network). One of the easiest ways to track this information down is through the website *Whois* (www.whois.com).

Whois is an online database that contains all the domain names that have been registered, including information about the person, organization, or company that has registered the domain. When someone registers a domain name, that person must provide contact information to *Whois*. Once it appears in the *Whois* database, that contact information becomes publicly available. The results of entering the web address for the company Uber into the *Whois* database are shown in figure 9.2.

As figure 9.2 indicates, the site is registered to www.markmonitor .com. If you leave the *Whois* site for a moment (and read laterally!) to look up MarkMonitor, you will find out that it is a company that protects the privacy of web domain owners. In fact, if you search many popular domains, including www.facebook.com, the same contact will come up. This contact appears because the registrant wants to maintain privacy and has chosen an option during the registration process that guarantees domain privacy. While you may not be able to find out everything you wanted to know about the site's owner, you can get a sense of how many domains belong to that owner. The site www.spyonweb.com can help. If we continue with the Uber example and we enter the domain address in *SpyOnWeb*, we find that all the other domains owned by the same domain owner are listed (fig. 9.3).

While *Whois* did not give us the information we needed because the website owner's privacy is protected, if we move laterally across the web and use another tool, we learn a bit more. At the very least, we determine that www.uber.com is the legitimate site for this company and not a fraud or phishing site. Although the usefulness of *Whois* will depend on your project and goals, you can use it as needed to provide additional information about your sources.

uber.com

Domain Information

Domain:	uber.com
Registrar:	MarkMonitor Inc.
Registered On:	1995-07-14
Expires On:	2028-07-12
Updated On:	2021-12-15
Status:	clientDeleteProhibited clientTransferProhibited clientUpdateProhibited
Name Servers:	dns1.p04.nsone.net dns2.p04.nsone.net dns3.p04.nsone.net dns4.p04.nsone.net edns126.ultradns.biz edns126.ultradns.com edns126.ultradns.net edns126.ultradns.org

Registrant Contact

Organization:	Uber Technologies, Inc.
State:	CA
Country:	US
Email:	Select Request Email Form at https://domains.markmonitor.com/whois/uber.com

Fig. 9.2. Results of entering the web address for the company Uber into the *Whois* database

Raw Whois Data

Domain Name: uber.com
Registry Domain ID: 2564976_DOMAIN_COM-VRSN
Registrar WHOIS Server: whois.markmonitor.com
Registrar URL: http://www.markmonitor.com
Updated Date: 2021-12-15T22:42:22+0000
Creation Date: 1995-07-14T04:00:00+0000
Registrar Registration Expiration Date: 2028-07-12T07:00:00+0000
Registrar: MarkMonitor, Inc.
Registrar IANA ID: 292
Registrar Abuse Contact Email: abusecomplaints@markmonitor.com
Registrar Abuse Contact Phone: +1.2083895770
Domain Status: clientUpdateProhibited (https://www.icann.org/epp#clientUpdat
Domain Status: clientTransferProhibited (https://www.icann.org/epp#clientTra
Domain Status: clientDeleteProhibited (https://www.icann.org/epp#clientDelet
Registrant Organization: Uber Technologies, Inc.
Registrant State/Province: CA
Registrant Country: US
Registrant Email: Select Request Email Form at https://domains.markmonitor.c
Admin Organization: Uber Technologies, Inc.
Admin State/Province: CA
Admin Country: US
Admin Email: Select Request Email Form at https://domains.markmonitor.com/wh
Tech Organization: Uber Technologies, Inc.
Tech State/Province: CA
Tech Country: US
Tech Email: Select Request Email Form at https://domains.markmonitor.com/who
Name Server: edns126.ultradns.org
Name Server: dns2.p04.nsone.net
Name Server: dns3.p04.nsone.net
Name Server: dns1.p04.nsone.net
Name Server: edns126.ultradns.biz
Name Server: edns126.ultradns.com
Name Server: dns4.p04.nsone.net
Name Server: edns126.ultradns.net
DNSSEC: unsigned
URL of the ICANN WHOIS Data Problem Reporting System: http://wdprs.internic.
>>> Last update of WHOIS database: 2022-02-08T13:01:39+0000 <<<

Fig. 9.3. Results of entering the web address for the company Uber into the *SpyOnWeb* database

Strategies for Locating Defunct Websites

According to Netcraft, an Internet services company, there are approximately 1.8 billion sites on the web ("January 2018 Web Server Survey"). Still, you may find yourself wanting to locate a site that is no longer available. The easiest way to find a defunct or inactive website is by using *Wayback Machine* (archive.org/web). The site has an easy-to-use interface and asks you to enter the web address you're looking for in a search bar

Fig. 9.4. Home page of *Wayback Machine*, which locates archives for defunct websites

on its home page (fig. 9.4). Its basic service is free and allows you to locate archived websites. Note that not all sites are archived by *Wayback Machine*, but many are.

⚙ TRY IT

1. Ponder the uses of reverse searches.

Why would you want to conduct a reverse search? What can a reverse search tell you?

2. Practice conducting a reverse image search.

Choose any image on the web. Conduct a reverse image search until you find the original image. What was the image's original context? Has the image been manipulated in any way? Explain.

3. Practice using fact-checking sites.

Using *Snopes* (www.snopes.com), investigate whether children have been fined for operating lemonade stands without a permit or if this allegation is a hoax. What did you find out?

4. Locate other fact-checking sites and determine their biases.

In the last few years, fact-checking sites have sprung up all over the web. Locate two fact-checking sites that are not listed in this chapter and determine their biases.

5. Determine hoaxes.

Using one of the fact-checking sites described in this chapter, determine whether Project MKUltra, also known as the CIA's mind-control program, is real or not. What did you find out?

Composing in Digital Spaces

RELATED APPENDIX ACTIVITIES: 3.3, 4.3

So far, this guide has taught you how to be a thoughtful and discerning user of digital technologies. But being digitally literate also means that you can use digital technologies to compose and create in productive ways both in your classes and in your personal life. You already compose daily in digital spaces. Every time you tweet, post on *TikTok* or *Instagram*, or send an e-mail you are composing in a digital space. This chapter addresses how you can use what you already know about composing in those digital spaces and apply it to digital projects you may be assigned in your classes.

Drawing on What You Already Know about Digital Composition

Each time you post on social media you are engaging in digital composition. While you may not think all that long and hard before you do so, you still likely put some thought into the creative and publishing process. We might even say that you have considered the rhetorical features of your post. For example, if you are posting a video, you've likely considered the *purpose* for creating and publishing the video, even if it's just to share a great makeup tip or cool trick your dog can do. You've also likely considered your *audience*. You know, for example, that you have certain followers on some of your social media accounts and different followers on others, and you've likely made a deliberate—even if quick—decision about the best platform to post on. While you may not be making an overt *claim* in your video, you're making at least a subtle one, such as "this makeup tip is great" or "this dog trick is cool." The *evidence* you are providing is the video itself. Finally, you've probably given some thought to the *design* of your video. At the very least, you have considered where to record the video, what kind of lighting you need, and where you will position your phone or other recording device in relation to yourself. Maybe you have even added some design features. In other words, not only do you already have practice in digital composition but, if you have read chapter 5 in this guide, the terms italicized throughout this paragraph are already familiar to you as the five rhetorical elements to pay attention to while engaging sources, including visual sources. As discussed throughout the rest of this chapter, those elements remain crucial as you create— rather than just consume—digital material.

Creating Multimodal Projects in Digital Spaces

Most digital compositions or projects are also multimodal. The word *multimodal* means more than one mode. There are five modes of communication:

- the linguistic mode, which conveys meaning through words and language
- the visual mode, which conveys meaning primarily through an image
- the aural mode, which conveys meaning through sound
- the spatial mode, which conveys meaning through layout
- the gestural mode, which conveys meaning through facial expressions and body language as well as through the ways the text might control how you navigate or interpret it

While almost all compositions are multimodal, some compositions privilege one mode over the other. For example, a traditional essay is in the linguistic mode, but the spatial mode is also represented through the paragraphing and other considerations regarding layout and spacing. A photograph is an example of a composition that conveys meaning through the visual mode, while a podcast is an example of a composition in the aural mode. A poem that is arranged on the page in a particular way is making use of the spatial mode in addition to the linguistic mode. An image of someone clutching their heart is making use of the gestural mode, as is a comic that uses cells to guide your reading process. Both of these examples are also making use of the visual mode.

Multimodal composing invites you to use various modes—rather than the traditional alphabetic essay in the linguistic mode—to develop and communicate your ideas. Print-based multimodal texts include comics, graphic novels, posters, and brochures. Digital multimodal texts include web pages, blogs, vlogs, films, videos, animation, and social media posts.

Composing multimodal texts in digital spaces further enhances your digital literacy skills. Multimodal projects give you the freedom to bring in multiple modes to help you develop and communicate your ideas to strengthen your projects. For example, maybe your instructor asks you to create a website that encourages newly turned eighteen-year-olds to vote in the upcoming presidential election. You might draw on several modes to do so. You could include patriotic music on the site (aural mode), images and photographs that portray the ideals of democracy (visual mode), and information about where to vote (linguistic mode). In creating the website, you may pay particular attention to your use of white space so that the different elements of the site really pop (spatial mode), and you might move your readers through the site by creating special effects that guide them in a particular direction (gestural mode). Compare this website project to a traditional essay that outlines the importance of voting in elections. While both formats have the same purpose, the website would likely be far more effective than an essay at encouraging eighteen-year-olds to vote.

Because the expectations of multimodal projects vary so much, this chapter does not attempt to teach you how to complete every multimodal project you may be assigned. Instead, drawing on the rhetorical features you were taught earlier in this guide to help you analyze sources, this chapter outlines what you should keep in mind as you complete multimodal assignments in digital spaces.

Rhetorical Considerations for Multimodal Composing in Digital Spaces

There are many kinds of multimodal compositions you might be asked to create. Your instructor may ask you to develop a blog, a website or web page, an infographic, a podcast, an essay with embedded images and hyperlinks, a digital portfolio, or any number of other digital compositions. Alternatively, you may be asked to remix or remediate one of your more traditional essays into a multimodal composition. As you compose in digital spaces, you will want to reflect on the rhetorical elements of your project to most productively reach your goals. You will recognize these rhetorical elements from chapter 5, where you received instruction in how to analyze these elements in compositions created by others. As the composer, you are now thinking about how these rhetorical elements can help you purposefully create projects addressed to specific audiences.

> **Purpose**. What is the purpose of your project? Are you making an argument? Are you educating or informing? Are you inciting some sort of action?
>
> **Audience**. Who are you trying to reach with your project? Your instructor? Specific ethnic groups? Adults? Children? A group of people that lives in a specific geographic region, eats a specific kind of food, or purchases certain items online?
>
> **Claims**. What argument or arguments might your project make? If the purpose of your project is to make an argument, your claims will be more recognizable. If, on the other hand, you have a different purpose, your claims may be more subtle or nonexistent.
>
> **Evidence**. What kind of support do your claims or your overall project call for? What kinds of sources, materials, or ideas do you need to bolster your purpose?
>
> **Design**. How can you design or arrange the elements of your project to highlight and further support your purpose?

There is an additional rhetorical element that is central to composing multimodal projects that has been raised throughout this chapter: genre. *Genre* is a fancy word for *kind*. The kind of project you choose to create (e.g., a podcast, infographic, photographic essay) will be linked to the rhetorical elements above, as you can see in the questions just below associated with genre.

Genre. Which genre will help you achieve your purpose and reach your audience? Which genre will help you highlight your claims and evidence in clear and precise ways? How can the design elements of specific genres help you reach your goals?

The infographic in figure 10.1, an example of a multimodal project, was created by a sophomore in college and published on a flyer for incoming students. In a reflection on how she integrated the five rhetorical elements, the student explains the following:

The purpose of my multimodal project is to inform students. Specifically, it is intended to remind incoming undergraduates of the guidelines they need to follow in face-to-face classes during the COVID-19 pandemic. Because incoming students are the audience and they would be receiving so many other materials at the start of the school year, I chose the genre of an infographic which presents condensed information in a way that is really easy and quick to read.

Additional Considerations for Composing in Digital Spaces

When you compose in digital spaces you will need to make informed and strategic decisions about everything from the tools you will use to how you will make your compositions accessible to the widest possible audience.

Choosing Digital Tools

You are already likely comfortable with various digital tools, and you should draw on that knowledge and experience while completing your projects. When working on academic projects, you need to think about which digital tools help you reach your personal goals for the assignment. This involves imagining how you are going to execute your project,

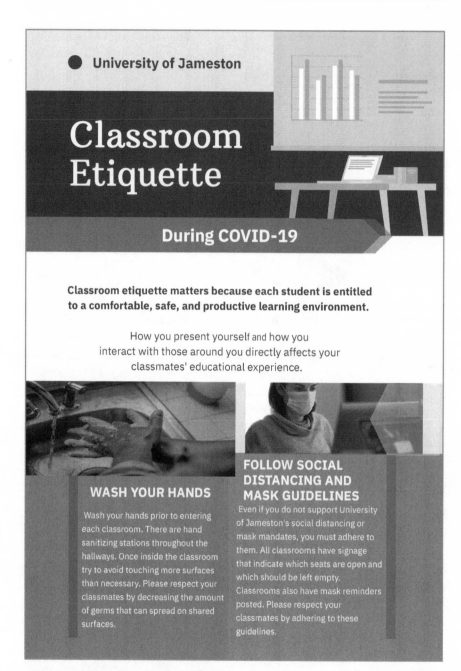

Fig. 10.1. Classroom etiquette infographic

including what you want to communicate and how you are going to communicate it. Then you want to consider which digital tools will help you do so. This means that you want to be sure you have access to and feel comfortable with the tools you plan to use.

Composing Ethically

As described in chapter 8, just as you must abide by the rules of academic integrity and avoid plagiarizing when you write a traditional essay, you need to do the same when developing multimodal projects. Many images, videos, and other elements are protected by copyright law, and you can't simply copy them into your project. That said, if you look a little harder, you will be able to find images and other materials that are under what is called Creative Commons (or CC) licensing, which means that you can reproduce these as long as you are not doing so for commercial purposes (i.e., to make money). Just as you are expected to avoid plagiarizing when composing in the traditional sense, you want to avoid infringing on copyright laws when you compose multimodally. You can do so by using images and other materials that fall under Creative Commons licensing and by citing all your images and visual sources. Your teacher may ask that you use the space underneath an image or graphic to cite your source and that you do so in the form of a caption. Alternatively, or in addition to that caption, your instructor may request that the citation appear at the end of your project on a designated references page.

Creating Accessible Compositions

To maximize the number of people who can engage with your composition, be sure to compose in accessible and inclusive ways. When using images, for example, include alternative text, or alt text. This short description of the image helps visually impaired users make sense of the image, which may not be explained by their screen readers or other devices they are using to accommodate their disability. Take some time to learn about which fonts and color schemes are most accessible and include different ways for audiences to engage with your compositions. If you embed a video, for example, also include a transcript.

Reflecting Regularly

Many multimodal projects are accompanied by a reflection in which you have the opportunity to describe your process for composing the project and the rationale for the choices you made while doing so. This is important work to complete at various stages throughout the composing process. Waiting until you are finished with your project to reflect on it means that if you have not met your personal goals or those of the assignment, you won't know until it's too late. Check in with yourself throughout the project to monitor your progress. Reflection is also important once you have completed your project because you have the opportunity to consider what you have learned while composing, how well you accomplished your personal goals for the project, and how well you met the goals of the assignment.

⚙ TRY IT

1. Identify the five modes of communication.

Name and define the five modes of communication and include an example of each.

2. Practice working with the modes of communication.

Create a short video in which you highlight the visual mode but also one of the other modes. Explain how that second mode functions.

3. Practice conveying a visual argument.

Take photographs and arrange them to make an argument. Explain what the argument is, its intended audience, and the ways in which you organized the photographs to make the argument and reach your intended audience.

4. Understand accessibility.

List two ways to make your multimodal compositions more accessible.

5. Define Creative Commons licensing.

Describe what a Creative Commons license is and how it might impact the sources you choose to include in your projects.

11

Customizing Your Online Experience

What you see on the web is filtered for you by algorithms, which you learned about in chapter 2. This final chapter explores how *you* can influence the filters and algorithms, particularly on social media platforms, to take more control of your online experience.

Adjusting Your Preferences

Social media platforms frequently redesign their user interface. *Snapchat*'s news feed, called Stories, for example, was redesigned in early 2018 so that items appear in chronological order. This change was made in response to complaints by users like you. So remember: when websites make undesirable changes that affect how you understand the information presented, you can take control of your online experience and make your voice heard.

In addition to making your preferences known, you can adjust your preferences. While there is no single way to adjust your preferences across social media platforms, *Twitter*, *Facebook*, *Instagram*, and other social media sites all have an area where you can adjust your privacy preferences. This tab or section is called something different across platforms, but the word *privacy* or the broader term *settings* is used to indicate where you need to go to control who can view your account. When it comes to the privacy of your social media accounts and posts, each platform has its own default setting. Some will default to the *public* designation, and it is up to you to change your preferences to make your account private. Some platforms have several options between public and private that allow you to further specify your preferences regarding who can access your page or posts. Finally, some social media platforms default to allowing third-party apps or organizations to view your account. You can also control this access through the privacy settings on the app or site.

Making Informed Decisions about Social Media Platforms

You have many choices when it comes to which social media platforms you use. While these platforms share many features, you may want to keep in mind that some platforms have acknowledged their role in the spread of fake news as well as in the related problems that arise from algorithms. In both cases, accurate and complete information may not be provided to you when you navigate social media sites. Some platforms have proudly announced their lack of fake news. As Max Chafkin, a reporter for *Bloomberg Businessweek*, describes, *Snapchat* "has found no evidence of political ad buys by anyone in Russia" and "appears to have no fake news at all." One senior executive at *Snapchat* explains the following: "We only work with authoritative and credible media companies, and we unashamedly have a significant team of producers, creators, and journalists" (Bell qtd. in Chafkin). Instead of relying on an "algorithm-driven News Feed," Chafkin explains, "Snapchat has taken a more old-fashioned approach. The app's news section . . . is limited to professionally edited content." *Snapchat*'s user-created videos "are vetted before they can reach a wide audience," and its feed of user-generated content is edited and fact-checked by staff members and reviewed by lawyers when necessary (Chafkin).

This kind of information about platforms is available by reading laterally across the web and is worth considering. Think about your values and priorities and whether the platform complements them. If trustworthy content is your priority, then find a platform likely to provide it.

Using Sharing, Liking, and Other Social Signals to Your Advantage

Another way to exert control over what is shown to you on social media platforms is to actively engage with the material. Each time you "like" a photograph or news story, for example, and even more so when you share something, you are telling the platform's algorithm that you would like to see more such items. To customize your experience, you should actively indicate what you like so you get to see more of it. Alternatively, when something comes across your screen that you don't like, don't share it, even if you are doing so to point out to a friend how much you disagree with it. The algorithm cannot discern *why* you have shared something. Instead, it assumes that sharing means that you want to see additional items like it.

While social media platforms are not always transparent about their algorithms, *Instagram* did share its algorithm, including the top three factors that determine what you see in your feed: whether the site predicts you'll be interested in a post, how new the post is, and how close you are to (that is, how much you interact with) the person sharing the post. Beyond those core factors, three additional signals that influence rankings are how frequently you visit the site, how many people you follow, and how long you spend on the site when you visit (Constine).

When social media platforms like *Instagram* share their algorithms, it's important to pay attention. Understanding how algorithms work makes you a more digitally literate and informed consumer and positions you to play a role in seeing more of what you would want to see and less of what you don't want to see.

By keeping up with announcements from social media platforms and indicating your preferences explicitly in the ways described in this chapter, you can help personalize the information, images, and other materials you view online. As *you* take control, you reduce the amount of control you have given to algorithms that would otherwise make these determinations for you.

Many believe that the kind of personalization described here leads to the filter bubbles and echo chambers outlined in chapter 2, which can seal people off from one another and undermine the very dialogue and consideration of diverse viewpoints on which democracy depends. Personalization is important because it empowers you, but you should still strive to create opportunities to engage with the perspectives and ideas of others.

Avoiding Clickbait

Clickbait is online content that tries to compel users to click on a related link. You won't see it called *clickbait* on your screen. Clickbait often appears under the titles *sponsored content* and *sponsored stories*. Because click-bait's main purpose is to attract attention rather than offer high-quality content, the term *clickbait* has acquired a negative connotation.

Clickbait uses various tactics. In some instances, clickbait appeals to your sense of curiosity through sensational headlines and striking images. For example, the clickbait shown in figure 11.1 tempts you to click to find out "what happens next." Clickbait often uses lists and numbers to attract your attention: the clickbait shown in figure 11.2 promises five things that will confirm your boyfriend is cheating on you. Clickbait often overpromises by claiming that you will gain knowledge or be shocked by clicking when, in fact, neither is likely to result. Sensational headlines and exaggerated promises are often indicators that you are seeing clickbait.

Clickbait often tries to sell you something or to generate ad revenue for the site, and clickbait manipulates images and provides misleading headlines that can lead you to believe falsehoods. At its worst, clickbait is a guise to steal your personal information and maybe even your iden-

Fig. 11.1. Example of clickbait

Fig. 11.2. Example of clickbait

tity. While clickbait is becoming more sophisticated and harder to distinguish from real content, avoiding clicking on such bait—no matter how curious you are—can reduce the amount of it you encounter. Certainly, clickbait is not going away anytime soon, but if you refrain from clicking on it or sharing it with others, it will not become popular enough to appear at the top of your social media pages.

✿ TRY IT

1. Ponder the value of customizing your online experience.

Consider what you read in this chapter and explain why you might want to customize your online experience. What are the benefits, if any, of doing so? Are there any drawbacks? If so, how can they be avoided?

2. Research social media platforms.

This chapter reviews the practices of various social media platforms. Choose a platform you use and research some of its practices by reading laterally about it. What did you find out? What did you already know about the platform? What surprises you?

3. Practice adjusting filters.

Go into one of your social media accounts and read about how you can adjust the various filters. Were you previously aware of all the adjustments you could make? Now that you know about these adjustments, are you inclined to make any? Why or why not? Adjust one of the filters to customize your online experience. Then track any differences you notice because of this adjustment. What did you find?

4. Develop clickbait headlines.

Review the samples of clickbait in this chapter (figs. 11.1 and 11.2). Go online and locate a few more examples. Then develop your own clickbait headlines. What characteristics of clickbait headlines did you choose to incorporate into your headlines?

5. Recognize how clickbait works.

Go online and locate five clickbait headlines. Write a sentence about each headline detailing why you think the headline would compel someone to click on it. For example, does the headline appeal to a user's emotions, and, if so, which emotions? Is the headline shocking? Does the headline promise some kind of reward?

Appendix: Sample Lesson Plans

Lesson Plan 1: Searching for Sources and Analyzing Their Credibility

This lesson plan brings together several of the skills covered in this guide. As such, students are expected to have read the guide before engaging in these activities. The learning outcomes for this lesson include the following:

- Students will learn about themselves as researchers by reflecting on their online searching habits.
- Students will be able to examine results from a *Google* search and speak to the different kinds of sources the search returns, including whether they are scholarly sources, wikis, personal websites, blogs, and so on.
- Students will be able to analyze sources for their credibility by reading laterally.
- Students will be able to track down any primary documents or sources relevant to the subject.

Introduction to the Lesson

This lesson opens with an opportunity for students to write for five to ten minutes about how they search for information online. Students' reflections might focus on information searches they have conducted for academic projects or for personal reasons. Students might also address the differences—if any—between their search practices when conducting research for school and for personal reasons. This activity will help students understand their own practices and reveal what they already know (and don't know) about conducting online searches.

ACTIVITY 1.1

The instructor introduces a research topic or question (or decides on one with the class) that will serve as the example for the remainder of the lesson. Together, using *Google* (the most widely used search engine), the class conducts a search for that topic or question. The class then reviews each entry on the first three pages of results. Instructors may divide the class into three groups so that each group has one page. Alternatively, all students may work on the results from all three pages. Students may refer to figure 3.1 in chapter 3 as they engage in the activity.

Questions that should guide students' analysis of the results:

1. What kind of sources appear on the page (e.g., news sources, scholarly sources, wikis, blogs)?

2. What are the vetting practices associated with each kind of source (that is, are the sources reviewed, and by whom)?

This activity concludes with the students sharing their answers to the questions above and the instructor filling in any gaps that emerge during the discussion with relevant information from the guide.

RELEVANT CHAPTER: 3

ACTIVITY 1.2

Working alone, in pairs, or in small groups, students read laterally about two to three of the sources that were returned in the search. It is fine if some students focus on the same sources since this offers opportunities for them to compare their processes of reading laterally. To take their bearings, before they begin students should develop a short written plan for reading laterally about the source, its place of publication, and its author. Students take notes on what they find as they go, making sure to move purposefully from one source to the next. Students then share their processes and findings with the class. The instructor reviews or refers to sections of the guide that are relevant as the discussion proceeds.

RELEVANT CHAPTER: 6

ACTIVITY 1.3

Students practice locating primary sources mentioned in the links that the *Google* search returned in activity 1.1. Depending on the subject or research question, there may be few or many sources that refer to original documents (such as a scientific study, speech, or video). Students must scour the sources to find places where a primary source is mentioned or linked to. Working alone, in pairs, in small groups, or as a whole class, students track down the primary source. This activity concludes with a full-class review of the difference between primary and secondary sources and the benefits of working from primary sources.

RELEVANT CHAPTER: 5

Lesson Plan 2: Reading Sources

This lesson plan brings together several of the skills covered in this guide. As such, students are expected to have read the guide before engaging in these activities. The learning outcomes for this lesson include the following:

- Students will learn about their reading practices by reflecting on their reading habits.
- Students will be able to apply reading strategies to help them understand the content of their sources.
- Students will be able to recognize bias in sources.
- Students will be able to judge and describe the relevance of sources to a subject.

Introduction to the Lesson

This lesson opens with an opportunity for students to write for five to ten minutes about how they read. Students' reflections might focus on what they read, where they read, and whether they regularly annotate their reading or take notes in some other form as they read. Students might also address the differences, if any, between their reading practices when reading for school versus reading for pleasure. This activity will help students understand their own reading practices and reveal the strategies they may already have for making sense of what they read.

ACTIVITY 2.1

To complete this lesson, students must have at least one source to work with. This source might be one of those gathered in lesson plan 1, a source selected and distributed by the instructor, or one that students found and will be using for a research project. The instructor should choose one or two of the reading strategies from chapter 5 to focus on with students. Students should review the section "Strategies for Reading Texts" in chapter 5 about the reading strategy or strategies selected. Then, students read the source by applying the strategy or strategies. Depending on the strategy or strategies, students should be able to discuss what they found by reading in this way. For example, if students rhetorically read the source, they should be able to discuss its rhetorical elements and the rhetorical appeals it makes. If the students were asked to compose twenty-five-word summaries, they should share those. If the students were asked to develop a map representing the reading, they should share it. As students share their readings with the class, the instructor can expand the discussion by asking some of the following questions, which will help develop students' metacognitive awareness of the usefulness of these strategies.

1. Having applied [instructor names the strategy] to the source, do you think you understand what the source says? If so, what aspect of the strategy helped you achieve an understanding of the source? If not, why do you think the strategy failed?

2. Are there other strategies we did not practice but that you read about in the guide that you think might help you understand the source?

3. Are there texts outside this class that you think would be easier to read if you applied these strategies? Can you name specific texts or classes and why applying the strategies would be helpful?

RELEVANT CHAPTER: 5

ACTIVITY 2.2

As is the case with activity 2.1, students must have at least one source to work with to complete the activity. This activity works best, however, with two or more sources. With two to three sources on the same subject, students read the sources for bias. Using the discussion of bias in chapter 7 as a reference, students track the forms of bias (i.e., bias by omission, by selection of sources or experts, by emphasis) that they see in the sources as they compare their perspectives on the subject. As they do so, students also describe the features of the source that reveal this bias (i.e., overstatements and generalizations, loaded words, labeling). The class discusses its findings, and the instructor reviews any relevant sections from chapter 7 of the guide.

RELEVANT CHAPTER: 7

ACTIVITY 2.3

This activity asks students to read for relevance. With a hypothetical (or real) research question or topic in mind, ask students to return to the sources they just read for bias in activity 2.2. Now ask them to read for relevance. With their research question or topic in mind and using the list of the ways that a source may be relevant from chapter 4, students write a paragraph about how each source might be relevant to their research question or topic. Students share their findings with one another, and the instructor concludes the discussion by reviewing the concept of relevance with students.

RELEVANT CHAPTER: 4

Lesson Plan 3: Exploring the Concept of Fake News

This lesson plan brings together several of the skills covered in this guide. As such, students are expected to have read the guide before engaging in these activities. The learning outcomes for this lesson include the following:

- Students will be able to articulate and reflect on what they already know about fake news.

- Students will be able to describe the complexities that characterize the concept of fake news.
- Students will be able to develop a working definition of fake news.
- Students will be able to write a source-based essay on the subject of fake news.

Although this lesson culminates in a source-based essay and potentially a remix of that essay, activities 3.1 and 3.2 can be assigned as a sequence that does not lead to activity 3.3, the source-based essay. Alternatively, activities 3.1 and 3.2 can be used as stand-alone lessons.

Introduction to the Lesson

This lesson opens with an opportunity for students to write for five to ten minutes about what they know about fake news. Students' reflections might focus on where they have heard the term *fake news*, what they have heard about it, and what they think about it. They may also consider whether they think fake news matters and for whom.

ACTIVITY 3.1

Students reread "A Real History of Fake News" in chapter 7 and then read widely through sources on the World Wide Web about the concept of fake news. Students might also conduct a search for the term *fake news* in the library's catalog and databases, although this search will likely be less successful even if it does produce some early uses of the term. Students synthesize these sources to represent the complexity of the concept of fake news. Questions that might guide their inquiry into fake news include the following:

1. How does each source define fake news? Where do these definitions converge and diverge?
2. What kinds of bias play into how the sources define fake news? Where can this bias be detected?
3. Do the sources offer terms other than *fake news* to describe the same concept? If so, why? What are these terms?

Students can answer these questions alone, or the answers to these questions can become part of a more formal annotated bibliography or similar assignment. Students can compare their findings with classmates or continue this work outside class.

RELEVANT CHAPTERS: 4, 7

ACTIVITY 3.2

Using the sources they located in activity 3.1, students develop their own working definition of fake news. Students articulate to the class or in writing how they came to this definition, what they chose to include in the definition, and what they chose to leave out. Students also address how their definition compares with the definitions put forth by the published sources. If students move on to writing the formal essay (activity 3.3), this definition should be used there.

RELEVANT CHAPTERS: 4–8

ACTIVITY 3.3

Students compose a formal, source-based essay on the concept of fake news by developing a research question or line of inquiry within the broader subject of fake news. Students explore this specific question or line of inquiry through sources, using the skills for locating and evaluating sources covered in this guide. Some of the questions that might inform students' writing include the following:

1. What is the history of fake news? To what extent does this history matter?

2. For whom and what is fake news a problem? What are its consequences?

3. Does the term *fake* adequately represent the phenomenon? Are there other descriptors that are more relevant, accurate, or effective?

4. Can you imagine solutions to the problem of fake news? What would these solutions look like, who is responsible for developing them, and why should they be developed?

As part of this activity, you can also ask students to remix or remediate their source-based essay into another mode for a specific audience. Depending on their audience, students might choose to compose collages or infographics that condense material, thereby allowing audiences to process it quickly. Alternatively, creating a podcast, which is in the aural mode, would give students the opportunity to experience how the linguistic mode (i.e., the script for the podcast) and the aural mode work together. No matter the mode students choose, they should reflect on the shift from the primarily linguistic mode of the source-based alphabetic essay to the new mode, including why they chose the mode they did as well as the affordances (benefits) and limitations of the new mode.

RELEVANT CHAPTERS: 4–8, 10

Lesson Plan 4: Understanding Algorithmic Bias and Personalization

This lesson highlights the attention this guide has paid to the ethics of algorithms and allows students to explore firsthand how algorithmic personalization and bias work. The learning outcomes for this lesson include the following:

- Students will be able to articulate and reflect on what they already know about algorithms.
- Students will be able to describe what algorithms are, how they function, and the relationships between cultural and systemic biases and those that appear in algorithms.
- Students will be able to demonstrate through their own online searches, and comparisons with their classmates' searches, how algorithms work.
- Students will be able to write a source-based essay or compose a project in the visual mode on the subject of algorithmic bias.

Although this lesson culminates in an essay or visual project, activities 4.1 and 4.2 can be assigned as a sequence that does not lead to activity 4.3, the project. Alternatively, activities 4.1 and 4.2 can be used as standalone lessons.

Introduction to the Lesson

This lesson opens with an opportunity for students to write for five to ten minutes on what they already know about algorithms. This knowledge may come from the reading they have completed in this guide, from other texts, and from their experiences using search engines and visiting various websites. Students' reflections might also focus on whether they think algorithmic personalization and bias are a problem and for whom.

ACTIVITY 4.1

Students conduct a series of *Google* searches using the same search terms. They might try searches for "best book," "job openings," and "news." Students answer the following as they conduct the search:

1. Did autofill offer suggestions when you began typing? If so, for what? To what extent do these suggestions reflect earlier searches you have conducted?

2. What are the first five results for each search term? To what extent do these reflect earlier searches you have conducted?

Ask students to switch to the search engine *DuckDuckGo*, conduct the same searches, and answer the same questions. Once students have conducted the searches on both *Google* and *DuckDuckGo* and answered the questions above for each, put students in small groups and have them compare their results and answer the following questions:

1. How do your results from the *Google* searches compare with one another?

2. How do your results from the *DuckDuckGo* searches compare with one another?

3. How can you make sense of the differences and similarities you notice?

RELEVANT CHAPTER: 2

ACTIVITY 4.2

To complement students' experience with algorithms in activity 4.1, ask students to read and view some of the widely available sources on the World Wide Web (e.g., articles, TED talks) about algorithms and search engine bias. Ask students to write a short response about how their experiences converge and diverge with what experts have to say about algorithms. For example, in what ways do these experts' theories capture students' experiences and where do they fail to do so?

RELEVANT CHAPTERS: 2–8

ACTIVITY 4.3

Students compose a formal, source-based alphabetic essay or a project in a visual mode—such as an infographic, collage, or photo essay—on algorithmic bias by developing a specific line of inquiry within this broader subject. Students explore this specific question or line of inquiry using the material in this guide to support their composition, whether alphabetic or in one of the visual modes listed. Some of the questions that might inform students' compositions include the following:

1. Is algorithmic bias a problem? If so, for whom and why? What are its consequences? If it's not a problem, why not?

2. Where does algorithmic bias come from? What is its source?

3. Can you imagine ways to address and potentially mitigate or totally erase algorithmic bias? What would these mitigation tactics look like, who is responsible for developing them, and are they worth developing?

RELEVANT CHAPTERS: 2–8, 10

Works Cited

"About." *Media Matters for America*, www.mediamatters.org/about. Accessed 17 Sept. 2018.

"About NewsBusters.org." *NewsBusters*, www.newsbusters.org/about. Accessed 17 Sept. 2018.

Balatsoukas, Panos, and Ian Ruthven. "An Eye-Tracking Approach to the Analysis of Relevance Judgment on the Web: The Case of Google Search Engine." *Journal of the American Society for Information Science and Technology*, vol. 63, no. 9, Sept. 2012, pp. 1728–46.

Blakeslee, Sarah. "The CRAAP Test." *LOEX Quarterly*, vol. 31, no. 3, pp. 6–7, commons .emich.edu/cgi/viewcontent.cgi?article=1009&context=loexquarterly.

"Bot, *N.* (1)." *Merriam-Webster*, www.merriam-webster.com/dictionary/bot. Accessed 11 Jan. 2022.

Breakstone, Joel, et al. *Students' Civic Online Reasoning: A National Portrait.* Stanford History Education Group, 14 Nov. 2019, stacks.stanford.edu/file/druid:gf151 tb4868/Civic%20Online%20Reasoning%20National%20Portrait.pdf.

Brenan, Megan. "Americans Remain Distrustful of Mass Media." *Gallup*, 30 Sept. 2020, news.gallup.com/poll/321116/americans-remain-distrustful-mass-media.aspx.

Britton, Bianca. "Deepfake Videos of Tom Cruise Went Viral. Their Creator Hopes They Boost Awareness." *NBC News*, 5 Mar. 2021, www.nbcnews.com/tech/tech-news /creator-viral-tom-cruise-deepfakes-speaks-rcna356.

Burke, Kenneth. *The Philosophy of Literary Form.* 3rd ed., U of California P, 1974.

Carillo, Ellen C. *A Writer's Guide to Mindful Reading.* WAC Clearinghouse / UP of Colorado, 2017, wac.colostate.edu/books/practice/mindful/.

Chafkin, Max. "How Snapchat Has Kept Itself Free of Fake News." *Bloomberg Businessweek*, 26 Oct. 2017, www.bloomberg.com/news/features/2017-10-26/how -snapchat-has-kept-itself-free-of-fake-news.

Chaykowski, Kathleen. "Zuckerberg Defends Facebook's Role in Election but 'Regrets' Dismissing Impact of Fake News." *Forbes*, 27 Sept. 2017, www.forbes.com/sites/ kathleenchaykowski/2017/09/27/zuckerberg-defends-facebooks-role-in-election -but-regrets-dismissing-impact-of-fake-news/.

Constine, Josh. "How Instagram's Algorithm Works." *TechCrunch*, 1 June 2018, techcrunch.com/2018/06/01/how-instagram-feed-works/.

Craig, Jacob W. "Navigating a Varied Landscape: Literacy and the Credibility of Networked Information." *Literacy in Composition Studies*, vol. 5, no. 2, 2017, licsjournal.org/index.php/LiCS/article/view/739.

@DFRlab. "#BotSpot: Twelve Ways to Spot a Bot." *Medium*, 28 Aug. 2017, medium.com /dfrlab/botspot-twelve-ways-to-spot-a-bot-aedc7d9c110c.

Digital Literacy Task Force. "Digital Literacy, Libraries, and Public Policy." *American Library Association*, Jan. 2013, alair.ala.org/handle/11213/16261.

Essaid, Rami. "Commentary: The War against Bad Bots Is Coming. Are We Ready?" *Fortune*, 26 Feb. 2018, fortune.com/2018/02/26/russian-bots-twitter-facebook -trump-memo/.

Federal Aviation Administration. "Sport Parachuting." Advisory Circular 105-2E. *Federal Aviation Administration*, United States Department of Transportation, 4 Dec. 2013, www.faa.gov/documentlibrary/media/advisory_circular/ac_105-2e.pdf.

Georgas, Helen. "Google vs. the Library: Student Preferences and Perceptions When Doing Research Using Google and a Federated Search Tool." *Libraries and the Academy*, vol. 13, no. 2, Apr. 2013, pp. 165–85.

Gillespie, Tarleton. "Platforms Intervene." *Social Media + Society*, vol. 1, no. 1, Apr.–June 2015, journals.sagepub.com/doi/pdf/10.1177/2056305115580479.

Granka, Laura A., et al. "Eye-Tracking Analysis of User Behavior in WWW Search." *Proceedings of the Twenty-Seventh Annual International Association for Computing Machinery Special Interest Group on Information Retrieval Conference on Research and Development in Information Retrieval*, edited by Mark Sanderson et al., Association for Computing Machinery, 2004.

Hamilton, Kevin, et al. "A Path to Understanding the Effects of Algorithm Awareness." CHI Conference, 26 Apr.–1 May 2014, Toronto, social.cs.uiuc.edu/papers/pdfs/ paper188.pdf.

"Information Literacy." *UNESCO*, www.unesco.org/new/en/communication-and -information/access-to-knowledge/information-literacy/. Accessed 22 Feb. 2019.

"Information Literacy Competency Standards for Higher Education." *American Library Association*, 18 Jan. 2000, alair.ala.org/handle/11213/7668.

"Internet Bot." *Techopedia*, www.techopedia.com/definition/24063/internet-bot. Accessed 22 Feb. 2019.

"January 2018 Web Server Survey." *Netcraft*, 19 Jan. 2018, news.netcraft.com/ archives/2018/01/19/january-2018-web-server-survey.html.

Lord, Charles G., et al. "Biased Assimilation and Attitude Polarization: The Effects of Prior Theories on Subsequently Considered Evidence." *Journal of Personality and Social Psychology*, vol. 37, no. 11, 1979, pp. 2098–109.

Lyons, Benjamin A., et al. "Overconfidence in News Judgments Is Associated with False News Susceptibility." *Proceedings of the National Academy of Sciences*, vol. 118, no. 23, 2021, e2019527118, https://doi.org/10.1073/pnas.2019527118.

Manjoo, Farhad. "Welcome to the Post-text Future." *The New York Times*, 2 Feb. 2018, www.nytimes.com/interactive/2018/02/09/technology/the-rise-of-a-visual -internet.html.

McClure, Randall. "Googlepedia: Turning Information Behaviors into Research Skills." *Writing Spaces*, vol. 2, 2011, pp. 221–41, wac.colostate.edu/books/writing spaces2/mcclure--googlepedia.pdf.

Miller, Richard E. "On Digital Reading." *Pedagogy*, vol. 16, no. 1, 2016, pp. 153–64.

MLA Handbook. 8th ed., Modern Language Association of America, 2016.

Mosseri, Adam. "Bringing People Closer Together." *Facebook Newsroom*, 11 Jan. 2018, newsroom.fb.com/news/2018/01/news-feed-fyi-bringing-people-closer -together/.

Murphy, Mike. "Mark Zuckerberg Admits He Underestimated Impact of Fake News on Facebook." *MarketWatch*, 27 Sept. 2017, www.marketwatch.com/story/mark -zuckerberg-admits-he-underestimated-impact-of-fake-news-on-facebook-2017 -09-27.

Nickerson, Raymond S. "Confirmation Bias: A Ubiquitous Phenomenon in Many Guises." *Review of General Psychology*, vol. 2, no. 2, 1998, pp. 175–220.

Nightingale, Sophie J., et al. "Can People Identify Original and Manipulated Photos of Real-World Scenes?" *Cognitive Research: Principles and Implications*, vol. 2, no. 30, 2017, https://doi.org/10.1186/s41235-017-0067-2.

Noble, Safiya Umoja. *Algorithms of Oppression: How Search Engines Reinforce Racism*. New York UP, 2018.

O'Connell, Brian. "Lyft vs. Uber: Which Is Best for Riders and Drivers in 2018?" *The Street*, 27 Nov. 2018, www.thestreet.com/technology/lyft-vs-uber-14791376.

O'Neil, Cathy. "The Era of Blind Faith in Big Data Must End." TED2017, Apr. 2017, www.ted.com/talks/cathy_o_neil_the_era_of_blind_faith_in_big_data _must_end?language=en.

Pariser, Eli. *The Filter Bubble: What the Internet Is Hiding from You*. Penguin, 2011.

Petersen, Michael Bang. "Evolutionary Political Psychology." *The Handbook of Evolutionary Psychology*, edited by David M. Buss, Wiley, 2016, pp. 1084–102.

Purdy, James P. "Why First-Year College Students Select Online Research Resources as Their Favorite." *First Monday*, vol. 17, no. 9, 3 Sept. 2012, firstmonday.org/article /view/4088/3289.

Raichur, Arvind. "Filter Bubbles: Taking Back Our Social Media Control." *Adweek*, 4 Jan. 2018, www.adweek.com/digital/arvind-raichur-mrowl-guest-post-filter -bubbles/.

Silverman, Craig. "This Analysis Shows How Viral Fake Election News Stories Outperformed Real News on Facebook." *BuzzFeed*, 16 Nov. 2016, www.buzzfeed .com/craigsilverman/viral-fake-election-news-outperformed-real-news-on -facebook.

Silverman, Craig, and Lawrence Alexander. "How Teens in the Balkans Are Duping Trump Supporters with Fake News." *BuzzFeed*, 3 Nov. 2016, www.buzzfeed.com/ craigsilverman/how-macedonia-became-a-global-hub-for-pro-trump-misinfo.

Smith, Aaron. "Many Facebook Users Don't Understand How the Site's News Feed Works." *Pew Research Center*, 5 Sept. 2018, www.pewresearch.org/fact-tank/2018/ 09/05/many-facebook-users-dont-understand-how-the-sites-news-feed-works/.

Solon, Olivia. "The Future of Fake News: Don't Believe Everything You Read, See or Hear." *The Guardian*, 26 July 2017, www.theguardian.com/technology/2017/jul/ 26/fake-news-obama-video-trump-face2face-doctored-content.

Steinmetz, Katy. "The Dictionary Is Adding an Entry for 'Fake News.'" *Time*, 27 Sept. 2017, time.com/4959488/donald-trump-fake-news-meaning/.

Sweeny, Kate, et al. "Information Avoidance: Who, What, When, and Why." *Review of General Psychology*, vol. 14, no. 4, Dec. 2010, pp. 340–53.

Tal, Aner. "Beware the Truthiness of Charts." *Harvard Business Review*, 19 Nov. 2015, hbr.org/2015/11/beware-the-truthiness-of-charts.

Taylor, Jim. "Cognitive Biases v.s. Common Sense." *Psychology Today*, 18 July 2011, www.psychologytoday.com/us/blog/the-power-prime/201107/cognitive-biases -vs-common-sense.

Tufekci, Zeynep. "The Real Bias Built In at Facebook." *The New York Times*, 19 May 2016, www.nytimes.com/2016/05/19/opinion/the-real-bias-built-in-at -facebook.html.

Vosoughi, Soroush, et al. "The Spread of True and False News Online." *Science*, vol. 359, no. 6380, Mar. 2018, pp. 1146–51, https://doi.org/10.1126/science .aap9559.

Wardle, Claire. "Fake News. It's Complicated." *Medium*, 16 Feb. 2017, medium.com/1st -draft/fake-news-its-complicated-d0f773766c79.

———. "Stop Calling It Fake News: Information Disorder Is Complex, but Fixing It Starts with Calling It What It Actually Is." Interview with Matt Cadwallader. *Harvard Kennedy School PolicyCast*, 31 Jan. 2018, hkspolicycast.org/stop-calling-it -fake-news-6c86f9647e63.

Weir, Kirsten. "Why We Believe Alternative Facts." *Monitor on Psychology*, vol. 48, no. 5, May 2017, www.apa.org/monitor/2017/05/alternative-facts.aspx.

White, Lawrence T. "Is Cognitive Dissonance Universal?" *Psychology Today*, 28 June 2013, www.psychologytoday.com/us/blog/culture-conscious/201306/is -cognitive-dissonance-universal.

Wineburg, Sam, and Sarah McGrew. *Lateral Reading: Reading Less and Learning More When Evaluating Digital Information.* Stanford History Education Group Working Paper 2017-A1. *SSRN*, 9 Oct. 2017, papers.ssrn.com/sol3/papers.cfm?abstract_id =3048994.

Wineburg, Sam, et al. "Evaluating Information: The Cornerstone of Civic Online Reasoning." *Stanford Digital Repository*, 22 Nov. 2016, purl.stanford.edu/ fv751yt5934.

Zuckerberg, Mark. "I want to respond to President Trump's tweet. . . ." *Facebook*, 27 Sept. 2017, www.facebook.com/zuck/posts/10104067130714241.

Index

Page references in italics refer to content appearing in figures.